"God is Love - He never actually created us to die."
Copyright © 2021 Sylvie LaBerge.

All rights reserved. No part of this publication may be reproduced, distributed, or transmitted in any form or by any means, including photocopying, recording, or other electronic or mechanical methods, without the prior written permission of the publisher, except in the case of brief quotations embodied in critical reviews and certain other noncommercial uses permitted by copyright law. For permission requests, write to the publisher, addressed "Attention: Permissions Coordinator," at the address below. Although the author and publisher have made every effort to ensure that the information in this book was correct at press time, the author and publisher do not assume and hereby disclaim any liability to any party for any loss, damage, or disruption caused by any of the content, or errors, or omissions, whether such content or errors or omissions result from negligence, accident, or any other cause. The reader is also held responsible for making their own decisions and choices based on their own revelation that they personally have received and believe from the Holy Spirit.

ISBN 9798598307564

Book design by Feline Graphics.

God is LOVE
He Never Actually Created Us To Die

That is such
GOOD NEWS

Sylvie LaBerge

Contents

Appreciation	7
Preface	9
Foreword	11
Chapter One - His Love Eliminates Our Death Mentality	12
Chapter Two - We Are As He Is…On Earth Today	52
Chapter Three - Hard Questions – Easy Answers	70
Chapter Four - The Truth Sets Us Free	100
Chapter Five - Science Confirms The Word	126

Appreciation

I sincerely and whole heartedly thank almighty God for entrusting me with the task of writing this inspiring book. I do not take His grace lightly.

I also want to thank my kind, caring and loving husband, who has always supported me in my pursuit for what God has been calling me to do for over twenty-five years.

He doesn't always understand (he is more conservative in his spiritual beliefs) but he never once forbid me to not follow my calling. This book would never have been made possible without his amazing kind heart, love, and support. I love you so much!

I also want to thank my Dad, who forever continues to be my number-one cheerleader. Even though at times the revelation I share with him seems so foreign. He is always kind and supportive. I love you Dad.

I'm also very thankful for so many other people. You know who you are. My beautiful family (and extended family) and my amazing friends. Thank you so much for loving me as I am, even though at times it's hard to believe what I believe. Love you all.

Good News!

LOVE never fails.

1 Corinthians 13:8a (NIV)

Preface

I NEVER imagined that it would ever be on my radar to be called to write a book.

However, for the past several years I kept having a very deep desire to know more of His truth. I found that when truths were revealed I was thankful but I was also grieved to see so many people living in deception and turmoil. When all along God's desire for them is to live an abundant and prosperous life.

Our culture has been wired to believe what medical science and society dictates regarding:

- life expectancy
- peace
- joy
- healing
- prosperity etc.

I was seeing how we truly believe what the world says rather than what God's Word tells us. As time went on, I kept feeling a deeper desire to help in a more profound way.

So, when the idea for a book started dripping through the crevices of my mind, I felt that I had already been getting prepared.

Then, when I woke up one Saturday morning, I had the download in my spirit for the entire book. I knew what it was going to be called and what the chapter titles were going to be. So, I stepped out by faith and I'm genuinely amazed how it all came together. Although challenges peeped in, God always had the answers for me. Especially, when I wanted to give up because I was feeling so overwhelmed. It's incredible how He orchestrated so many details to make it all possible in such a short period of time. He has such a great sense of humor. Everything got done in just a few months even with the hectic demands of my full-time corporate job.

I'm glad that the sacrifice is not in vain. People from all different denominations, religions, spiritual and non-spiritual beliefs have already caught some deep insight from this thought-provoking, encouraging and life-changing book... and they love it!

Without a shadow of a doubt, I believe that it is God's will for this message to be released, now!

I believe your life will be enhanced through the decrypted layers of truth that you will find in each chapter, and I know you will want to read it over and over again.

Friend, it's not a coincidence that you are reading this now, so do not allow this opportunity to pass you by. Expect an amazing life-transforming experience and I'm confident you'll not be disappointed.

Then you will know the truth and the truth will set you FREE -John 8:32 (NIV)

Dedicated to Kayleigh M., Joyce, Dave, Laurie, Matt, Mike H., Joel, Victoria, Joseph P., Andrew W., Sid R., Bill J., Kris V. and Eric M.
God has blessed you all with a big platform. Thank you for all that you do to advance His Kingdom. I pray and challenge you to release the truths that He reveals to each one of you personally in this book, during this season. Thank you so much!

Foreword

God is Love and He Never Actually Created You to Die is an important book that people must read to break free from false mindsets that have kept them from accessing all the blessings in the Kingdom of God. The book has a refreshing interpretation of Scriptures which reveals the truth about God's design for immortality.

Sylvie LaBerge's delightful, charismatic, and joyful nature comes through as artfully in her writing as it does in conversations with her. Reading this work reveals her powerful connection with our loving Father God and opens up an avenue for you to deepen your connection with the Lord and His love for you.

I highly recommend every Christian to not only read this book but to embrace the truth shared here. As you do so, you will step into a world that God intended from the start - you will experience the Kingdom of God on earth.

Darlene A. Mayo, M.D.

Neurosurgeon and Neuroscientist
Author, The Science of God's Healing Power
www.drdarleneamayo.com

God's love for us is supernatural.

ONE

His Love Eliminates Our Death Mentality

Today, we are reminded that God is love. His Word tells us He wants us to have an abundant life and that nothing is impossible with Him.

FOR
With
GOD <LOVE>
Nothing Shall Be
IMPOSSIBLE
LUKE 1:37 (KJV)

He mentions this repeatedly in His Word. *Beloved, I pray that you may prosper in all things and be in health, just as your soul prospers. 3 John 1:2 (NKJV).*

He also tells us He has defeated death. *But it has now been revealed through the appearing of our Savior, Christ Jesus, who has destroyed death and has brought life and immortality to light through the gospel. 2 Timothy 1:10 (NIV).*

As a great Father, He wants the best for all of us. So why are people sick and why do people die?

These are questions we think about and ask ourselves only to give up because we can never find the answers. We have more faith in what the world says; rather than what God's word tells us.

After searching for over twenty years to find answers to these questions, I have come to the conclusion that knowing His love is the key that opens up the realm for the answers. His love for us is above and beyond what we can ever think or imagine. He loves and adores us so much. *For God so loved the world that he gave his one and only Son, that whoever believes in him shall not perish but have eternal life. John 3:16 (NIV).*

For you created my inmost being, you knit me together in my mother's womb. I praise you because I am fearfully and wonderfully made; your works are wonderful; I know that full well. Psalm 139:13-14 (NIV).

And even the very hairs of your head are all numbered. Matthew 10:30 (NIV).

Praise be to the God and Father of our Lord Jesus Christ, who has blessed us in the heavenly realms with every spiritual blessing in Christ. Ephesians 1:3 (NIV).

We all have an amazing inheritance. So, why do we go around feeling so defeated?

Our inheritance is not based on our good or bad behaviors. It's based on what He's already done for us. It's such an amazing and beautiful gift.

So, why do we seem to wake up each day feeling like we are on a never-ending Ferris wheel ride, just going *around and around,* with the same continuous thought patterns? Day in and day out...why are we doing and saying the same things, thinking the same thoughts, believing the same things and expecting different results?

Why do we keep living with a "silent" death mentality? It's presented the moment a baby is born. We seem to automatically agree in our minds to place them on the same *"life and death chart,"* that we are already on which looks like a straight line with numbers (usually 1 to 100). We call newborns one day *OLD.* Then, the journey from birth to death begins by using the word "old" and making a silent agreement that death is the end result.

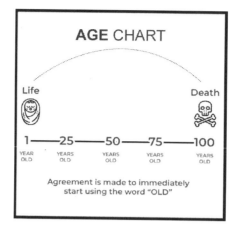

As life goes on, we eventually get to pick a number (age) that we hope and pray to reach before we die. These thoughts usually carry so much fear and anxiety because we are agreeing with death without even realizing it. We give death the power to enter into our lives as a strong foundational belief system.

Have you ever noticed how children's movies and books have animals and people that die? It's instilled in all of us at such a young age, without ever recognizing it... until now.

We need to understand that God is love. He operates differently than the ways of the world.

To put a special emphasis on who God is, you will notice He will be referred to in this chapter as *"God [love]."* He is the highest of all frequencies. In this frequency, there is healing, joy, peace, and abundant life. There is no death in Him. God is love and He is life. We've had so many distractions and deceptions that have kept us away from this truth. We have all believed too many lies. **The thief comes only to steal and kill and destroy; I have come that they may have life and have it to the full. John 10:10 (NIV).**

Praise be to the God and Father of our Lord Jesus Christ, who has blessed us in the heavenly realms with every spiritual blessing in Christ [the word of love]. Ephesians 1:3 (NIV).

So, what is going on? If we already have been blessed with all spiritual blessings with free access 24/7, to the realm of love (which is one with Him), why are we not experiencing what He is saying? The deeper we go into love, the more revelation (answers) we will receive.

God [love] tells us that without Him, we cannot do anything. *I am the vine; you are the branches. If you remain in me [love] and I in you, you will bear much fruit; apart from me [love], you can do nothing.* **John 15:5 (NIV).** Without love, we can't do anything. So, with love, we can do anything; nothing will be impossible. **Jesus looked at them and said, 'With man this is impossible, but with God [love] all things are possible. Matthew 19:26 (NIV).** We simply must have faith and believe what God [love] says.

To illustrate this further, we will look at the example of loving parents teaching their son about the miracle of apple seeds.

Looking at the seeds, they look so small and insignificant. It's challenging to explain to a child how those seeds will become apple trees. It makes no sense, just by looking at them. So, it's easy for the child to dismiss the idea. But if the child trusts his parents and if he has a loving relationship with them, he will believe what they tell him.

That trusting and loving relationship (based on love), will also affect this child's life, in many different ways. For example, the child will also trust his parents when they take him to the pool and they ask him to jump into their arms. Even though it looks scary and the water is way over his head and he can't even swim yet, he will still do it. He believes in what they tell him because he trusts them and he knows that his parents love him. He has faith in what they tell him. They've never lied to him, so he has no reason *not to believe* them. However, he will always have free will to change his mind. There will always be the choice to fear and to try to figure things out on his own and not to believe them.

So, it is with our Heavenly Father. He tells us to believe and to trust Him and that He will protect us from all evil. **Whoever dwells in** *the shelter of the most high [love] will rest in the shadow of the Almighty. I will say of the Lord [love], "He is my refuge and my fortress, my God, in whom I trust." Surely, he will save you from the fowler's snare and from the deadly pestilence. Psalm 91:1-3 (NIV).*

We have such a safe place in love [God]. Unfortunately, what happens too often, is that we fear and worry. We simply don't believe His Word. We try to figure things out on our own and as soon as something happens where we can't figure it out with our five senses, we withdraw from staying in faith, and we choose fear.

Once we tap into that negative energy, we tap into the frequency of death. We reap what we sow. What is so interesting, is that we will reciprocate back into our own lives, the same vibrations and frequencies that we think, speak, and believe.

Albert Einstein said, *"Everything is energy, and that's all there is to it. Match the frequency of the reality you want, and you cannot help but get that reality. It can be no other way."*

If you look at the following chart, you will see that whatever is currently present in your life is what you have chosen to tap into. To get rid of anything that is in the *death frequency,* just replace it with what's in the *life frequency*.

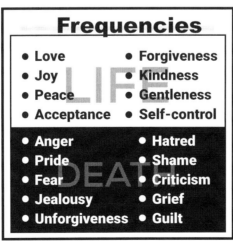

We just can't wish for things to go well – we have free will, and we get to make our own choices. We have been given authority on earth. God is not like a genie in a bottle that grants wishes or denies them. He's already provided in abundance all that we will ever need and desire and so much more.

When we choose love, our body chemistry reacts positively. However, when we speak sickness and death (even in the slightest forms), that's what we reap. Our words, emotions and thoughts are energy and frequency. We are continuously giving power to life or death.

We can't manipulate energy and frequency. If we choose to be worried and fearful, we will attract the same form of energy back into our circumstances and into our lives. Our bodies will also be affected. An overwhelming percentage of sickness and deaths are related to stress. God [love] reminds us to think of things that are true, pure, and of a good report. Being a Christian and wanting to reap an abundant life is not like a spectator sport, where we just get to watch and hope to win.

> **WHATEVER THINGS ARE**
> **TRUE**
> **HONORABLE**
> **RIGHT**
> **PURE**
> **LOVELY**
> **ADMIRABLE**
> **EXCELLENT**
> *and*
> **IF THERE IS ANYTHING PRAISE-WORTHY MEDITATE ON THESE THINGS**
>
> **PHILIPPIANS 4:8 (NKJV)**

We were all created to be victorious and we already have the victory.

But thanks be to God [Love] who gives us the victory through our Lord Jesus Christ [word of love]. 1 Corinthians 15:57 (NIV).
Once again, it is not based on our performance. It is based on what God [love] has done for us. He wants us to fellowship with Him [love] all the time, 24/7. He will never put us on hold and He's never too busy. He actually will never get fed up or discouraged with us and He remembers our sins no more. So, who are we to keep remembering them?

He tells us to forgive others. Why would He tell us to do such a thing? A big part of the answer is because when we choose not to forgive others, we are removing ourselves from the frequency of love. We then get to live the consequences of being apart from love (God) in that situation for our lives. When we are in that negative frequency, we are attracting the negative (death) back into our lives. We need to remain in love [God] to have a blessed life. It's been said, that it takes one moment to forgive or to ask for forgiveness, but unforgiveness will always remain a daily effort of negative energy that we will have to agree with every day, which will continuously reflect negativity back into our own lives. None of us would want that for our children, and neither does God [love] want that for us.

Unforgiveness, worry, and fear create a lot of stress. In fact, according to the previous chart, they are all in the death frequency. We have to change the way we think to His truth (life).

Let's look at the following example: When someone is born into a royal family, they don't need to worry about having food to eat or clothes to wear. We all agree with that way of thinking because we understand the protocol. We have mindsets and patterns of thinking that already agree that provision and a good inheritance are all part of what a royal family receives. Some people would call it a "no-brainer." Our Heavenly Father tells us the same thing.

"Therefore, I tell you, do not be anxious about your life, what you will eat or what you will drink, nor about your body, what you will put on. Is not life more than food and the body more than clothing?" Matthew 6:25 (ESV).

For us to worry and to be in fear is perhaps like telling God [love] that we don't trust Him and that we don't believe His Word. As soon as we make an agreement with those negative frequencies, we empower them into our lives.

Humble yourselves, therefore, under God's mighty hand, that he may lift you up in due time. Cast all your anxiety on him because he cares for you 1 Peter 5:6-7 (NIV). When we cast our cares on Him, we are humbling ourselves. The opposite is also true. When we are prideful, we don't cast our cares on Him. This can be such a huge life-changer.

Love (God) tells us not to tap into the negative frequencies of fear and worry. We are to speak His Word which is power and life. No matter what our five senses are telling us. *The tongue has the power of life and death, and those who love it will eat its fruit. Proverbs 18:21 (NIV).*

We face so many choices every day, and we get to continuously empower life or death by what we think and speak. Here is an example of Sammy; who is a young man that just lost his job several days ago.

When Sammy got up this morning, he had a choice to either speak what God's [love] Word says regarding his situation or to speak what is contrary. In other words, to speak life or death.

He had a choice to say, "Thank you God, for you are my provider. Thank you for guiding me to the perfect employment with a great boss and a great pay. Thank you, that I have the power to get wealth. I am blessed and I am a blessing."

Or, he had a choice to choose a defeated mindset based solely on how he feels and thinks. In this same scenario, when Sammy wakes up, he immediately dreads the day. He is already very discouraged and feels anxious. He just can't figure out how he will make ends meet. His agreement with the frequencies of worry and fear fuels the negative cycles, which attracts more of the same negative frequencies back into his life, which will then affect his health.

We know that the negative frequencies come to kill, steal, and destroy. So, we need to be mindful of our thoughts as they become our words, and our words manifest life or death in our life.

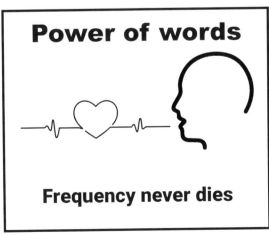

How do we stay in the love frequency, which is the way and the truth and the life? The power of gratitude is a huge key, along with making positive declarations from His Word and listening to praise and worship music. Taking a deep breath and seeing ourselves tapping back into love (God) is also amazing. Some of us call it the "Power of pause".

The more we know the truth, the more we will be set free. But we need to break old patterns of thinking and renew our minds to the truth. **So, then faith comes by hearing and hearing by the word of God. Romans 10:17 (NKJV).**

The fictional story of the elephants at a circus is a great example that illustrates the power of our minds. The scene is in Africa, and last year, they had a sweet new baby elephant that was born. Her name was Kena. The day after her birth, they put this precious baby elephant in a huge tent with her parents and relatives. One of her back legs was then gently chained to a small post, so she could not run away and set herself free. Throughout those next several weeks, she tried to free herself, but she quickly realized that she couldn't go anywhere because she was chained to the post. Seeing her parents and other relatives also chained to a similar post, reinforced her belief system; that this is just how it was supposed to be. It was the so-called "normal."

So, the elephants in this story live their entire lives with that same mindset and belief system. Even though when they would travel to various locations to perform in the circus, they could see from their trailer windows, that other elephants were living free in the wild. When they would see the other elephants free and happy, they felt very envious and discouraged. They just kept living their lives 'wishing and hoping' that they would have that same freedom and not always be all chained-up.

They also had numerous people speak to them and tell them pieces of the truth, but it always seemed way too good to be true. They rejected it all...thinking it was fantasy. The truth is they could have set themselves free. The jungle was always less than five hundred feet away. They just kept believing the lies in their minds and they kept following cycles (generational and traditional beliefs), which resulted in them being deceived and never exploring the truth for themselves.

So, it is with us. We've all had so many *patterns of this world* and different belief systems passed down to us from our parents, relatives, the media, teachers, pastors, etc., which mirrored a lot of what was passed down to them. Then one day, we realize that we are doing, saying, and believing the same things without ever having researched the truth for ourselves.

The good news is that once we learn there is more, we can seek the truth in His Word, and then through His Spirit, we find the higher truth. We are then able to break the old cycles of lies and replace them with new patterns of thinking. The truth is what sets us free. Becoming aware and starting to understand how crucial the frequency of love is and how all of our dreams and desires are in that realm; to include healing and an abundant long life is such a huge key. We then start making other choices that immediately affects our lives (physically and spiritually). We soon realize how impactful it will also be for countless generations to come. To really know that we are loved and that God (who is love) is always for us...changes everything! It brings life to a whole new level!

We need to take the time and listen to that small voice inside of us. He is always with us. We just need to tune into that frequency. **For indeed, the Kingdom of God is within you. Luke 17:21 (NKJV).**

It's in this place where we will hear our answers. They've always *all* been here for us. This is not anything that anyone can teach per say...because they are spiritually discerned.

Ask, and it will be given to you; seek, and you will find; knock, and it will be opened for you. For everyone who asks receives, and he who seeks finds, and to him who knocks it will be opened. Matthew 7:7-8 (NIV).

We can choose to ignore our spiritual self but it's a part of who we are. The battle is and always will be - the truth versus the lies. Basically, life verses death and there is no death in His Kingdom. We need to be awakened to this truth.

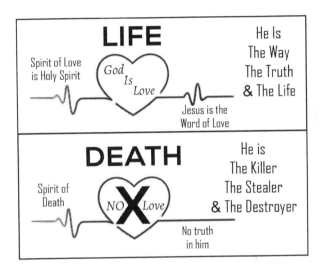

When we truly get to know God [love] and His character, we trust Him more. The more we trust Him, the more we get to experience His love. Even scientists have concluded that when we are in the frequency of love, our whole body reacts favorably, and healing occurs. With countless and endless studies, they also have concluded that the body is not made to die; it's always meant to heal itself.

Healing is in love. God is love. In love, there is no death. In love, there is no sickness. If we truly would believe the truth that all sickness has been eliminated, who would still be alive in your family line? So, what is causing most sickness? According to science, one of the biggest culprit is stress.

Here is another question: Is stress in the frequency of love? The answer is *no, it is not*.

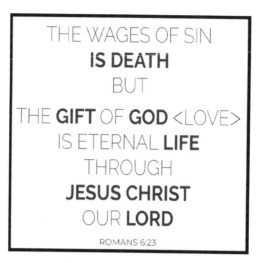

So, where is death in all of this? The short answer is that it is always **apart from love**.

Jesus, who is the Word of God [love], came so we could have life and have it abundantly. When Adam and Eve sinned, that was the beginning of the negative frequency in the world, and sin is what leads to death. Do you see?

When Jesus went to the cross, He took upon Himself *all our sins*. It was so much that He sweated blood as He took all the frequencies of sin and sickness - every disease that ever existed and that will ever exist. It was so much torture that He was unrecognizable. He did it all for you! He did it for all of us, so we would be set free. He did it all, to bring us back to the original state of love, where there is no sickness, and there is no death.

So now, we can live in the frequency of love, or we can go back and empower what He has already defeated. He gave us such a beautiful gift of abundant life, which includes no death. He already paid the full price. ***And which now has been manifested through the appearing of our Savior Christ Jesus, who abolished death and brought life and immortality to light through the gospel. 2 Timothy 1:10 (ESV). As He is, so are we in the world. 1 John 4:17 (KJV).***

Is there any sin in Him?

Is there any death in Him?

Is there a murder spirit in Him that wants to kill us?

I tell you, whoever believes in me will do the works I have been doing, and they will do even greater things than these, because I am going to the Father. John 14:12 (NIV).

Did He [love] raise the dead?

Did He [love] ever attend a funeral and watch them go six feet underground?

Did He [love] ever tell us we would physically die and that we would have to choose between being buried or cremated?

Did He [love] leave us instructions on how to mourn for loved ones?

Did He [love] ever make friends with death?

Did He [love] ever approve or make any agreement with death?

Did He [love] ever tell us to make agreement with death?

Would loving parents murder or kill their children (or make them sick), so they could all be with them in heaven? Of course, we would say "no." Well, neither would God, who is the perfect Father. So, why do people die? Why do they get sick?

Similar to the story of the elephant, we have been automatically programmed to think a certain way, which is to limit God. To even go against what He says, because we can't comprehend it with our five senses, or fit any of it into the patterns of our world. So, we have dismissed it and because we don't have a true loving relationship with our Heavenly Father, we rebel, unlike the child in the story of the 'apple seeds'.

APPLE **SEEDS**

The good news is that faith comes by hearing the Word of God, which is the truth, and the truth is what is setting us free; so, be very encouraged.

Therefore, I urge you brothers and sisters, in view of God's

mercy, to offer your bodies (5 senses) as living sacrifice. Holy and pleasing to God—this is your true and proper worship. Do not conform to the patterns of this world but be transformed by the renewing of your mind. Then you will be able to test and approve what God's will is - his good, pleasing, and perfect will. Romans 12:1-2 (NIV). Do you really believe that His perfect will is for you to become sick, suffer, and die?

Let's look at this again from a different angle. Do you believe that His perfect will for your loved ones is for them to become sick, suffer and die? Or, to cause everyone enormous pain and sorrow? Would a loving Father orchestrate all of that for you? Do you really believe that He wanted to take your loved ones that have already died, away from you, to cause you enormous grief and pain - not just once, but repeatedly, because He needed them in heaven?

Or, do you believe that...

- He really loves you?
- He wants the best for you?

- He doesn't want you to suffer?

- He doesn't want you to be sick?

- He doesn't want you or your loved ones to suffer and die?

You probably sense in your spirit that He does not want any death, but your mind is telling you it is impossible. For many of you reading this, you are feeling the tug-of-war between your flesh and your spirit. Your spirit always knows the truth, but your flesh wants to see and have it all figured out. So, who do you listen to? Who are you going to believe? Perhaps it goes back again, to our previous example of the loving parent in the 'apple seed' story. The child simply believes because he trusts his loving parents. Developing a relationship with our Heavenly Father [love], reading His Word, including Him in our everyday lives and seeking answers will bring more light to our personal questions and we will get our answers. God [love] will never ignore you. He loves you too much. ***If any of you lacks wisdom, you should ask God, who gives generously to all without finding fault, and it will be given to you. James 1:5 (NIV).*** As previously mentioned, we can all agree that an overwhelming amount of deaths are caused by sickness, and a huge percentage of sickness is caused by stress which is the body not at ease (dis-ease). His Word gives us the truth on how to stay at ease and at peace. ***You will keep in perfect peace those whose minds are steadfast, because they trust in you. Isaiah 26:3 (NIV).***

Science can now predict that living to be two hundred years of age or more will be possible very soon. There are some crazy computer enhancements that they are researching and experimenting with that will be linked to the human body, which will prevent the body from dying. So, if science can do this...God can, and He's already done so much more. So how do we live longer and forever? This is really a spiritual question with spiritual answers. As previously mentioned, we need to let go of our five senses (trying to figure it all out) and we need to see with our spiritual eyes and hear with our spiritual ears.

We simply need to seek Love and ask Him to show us the truth. Can it really be that simple? The answer is, "yes"!

But it has now been revealed through the appearing of our Savior, Christ Jesus, who has destroyed death and has brought life and immortality to light through the gospel. 2 Timothy 1:10 (NIV).

For whoever sows to please their flesh, from the flesh will reap destruction; whoever sows to please the Spirit, from the Spirit will reap eternal life. Galatians 6:8 (NIV). For many of us, we believe that our sins are forgiven, but when it comes to healing and immorality, it's challenging to change our thinking patterns to believe.

So, let's talk more about sickness (from a slightly different perspective) since this is such a big culprit for death. What is sickness? It's our cells and frequency not being aligned to the way they were originally designed to be; there is a malfunction. The frequency is off. **As he thinks within himself, so he is. Proverbs 23:7 (NASB)**. When we give power to the bad symptoms with our thoughts and words, we are then in agreement with the negative frequency. That doesn't result in healing, it's actually being in agreement with Satan (death). God's Word tells us, **but he was pierced for our transgressions, he was crushed for our iniquities; the punishment that brought us peace was on him, and by his wounds we are healed. Isaiah 53:5.** This was fully accomplished and it is available now, to anyone who believes.

What does all this mean? As stated, several times before (but worth repeating), He took all the negative frequencies which included the energy of sickness, and He bore it so we could be set free. He suffered, and His physical body died (He took all the death frequency called sin), and three days later, He rose from the dead. He defeated death for us. Your frequency was there. There are no time zones in the Heavenly realm. There is no past, present, and future. It's all outside of time.

For He chose us in him before the creation of the world to be holy and blameless in His sight. In love. Ephesians 1:4 (NIV). He knew you then. It's so confusing because we are programmed to think in the ways and patterns of the world, even when the subject of time is concerned. But in our spirits, we can ask Him to show us more and give us understanding. **Ask and it will be given to you; seek and you will find; knock and the door will be opened to you. Matthew 7:7 (NIV).**

Let's look at this again. He Himself bore our sins in His body on the tree that we might be free from sin and live in righteousness. By His wounds, we have been healed. Please take a moment and try to envision this scene and for the first time, look at the frequency and energy present in this event. Then, look at the third day when He rose again. What do you see?

That same power (frequency, energy, etc.) that you are trying to envision that raised Him from the dead (when He was all bruised and disfigured, etc.), that very same resurrection power lives in you. This is so huge. It's above and beyond what we can ever think or imagine. We have never truly believed it because our spiritual ears were not open, until now. Don't ever let go of this revelation - as it begins to open up more and more for you. Keep seeking the truth. **And if the Spirit of him who raised Jesus from the dead is living in you, he who raised Christ from the dead will also give life to your mortal bodies because of His Spirit who lives in you. Romans 8:11 (NIV).**

Many of us all over the world are starting to receive and gain more understanding of this amazing revelation, and the scales are being removed from our eyes. We can now see that God is love. With Him nothing is impossible! We do get to choose what we believe and what we limit. He is such a good Father. **Take delight in the Lord, and he will give you the desires of your heart. Psalm 37:4 (NIV).** He wants to give us the desires of our hearts.

It's no one's desire to suffer and to die. I don't know anyone who enjoys going to a funeral. When people are on their deathbed, it is a very sad time for them and for all their loved ones. It always leaves an incredible and painful void for those that are left behind. It's not what we were designed to be a part of. **That will never be a scene from a loving Father**. That is certainly not His will, He is not a murderer. Even when you were reading the sentences about the effects of death, you were probably sensing your frequency changing. It's because it is not in the realm of love. Do you see? Go back to it for a moment and try to see those frequencies. There is no love in them at all. It's all part of sin (death) which Jesus has defeated.

We need to believe what He says. **You, dear children, are from God and have overcome them, because the one who is in you is greater than the one who is in the world. 1 John 4:4 (NIV).**

Here is a great example of someone who believed that greater is He that was in him than he that is of this world. In the early 1900s, there was a man named John G. Lakes, who went to South Africa. A plague was killing thousands of people. He really believed that greater was Jesus in him than what was in that plague. So, scientists observed the causative (life) organisms of the plague in John's hand that would have normally killed any human; however, through specialized equipment, they saw that the plague was dying. It never killed him. He stood firm that greater was Jesus in him.

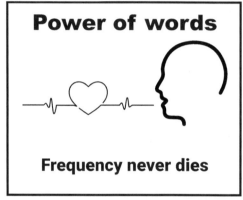

I believe that if we looked at the frequencies in and around our bodies, we would be blown away at the power of our minds and the power of our words. To quickly illustrate this concept, we can simply look at the placebo effect.

We've all heard the story about the two patients who went to the same doctor and their files were switched by mistake. One patient was told that he only had a certain number of months to live, and the other one was told that he was healed and that he would not die. Once they were given their results, their bodies reacted according to what they were told and what they believed. The patient that was told that he would live, indeed lived on. But the one who was told that he would die, actually died shortly thereafter. *For as a man thinks in his heart, so is he. Proverbs 23:7 (NKJV).*

Another interesting experiment occurred when scientists took two bowls of water in two different rooms. They spoke positive words and played nice harmonious music to one bowl. Then in another room, they spoke negative words and played music with harsh and unloving lyrics to the other bowl. They conducted this experiment for several weeks only to find out that the water in the bowl spoken to negatively, got polluted. While the water in the one spoken to positively remained clear. Our bodies are over fifty percent water. Do you see?

We have so much power. We always have a choice to speak and think life or death. We are continuously faced with choices that empower either one. As we have mentioned numerous times already, God, who is love, is the truth, the way, and the life. He is always available for us with no restrictions, whatsoever! We just need to accept Him and to want to develop a relationship with Him. One reason people are often tuned out of love is they think and believe that they have to earn the right. Or, they have taken offense because they don't understand why they are not experiencing His love in their lives - so they feel rejected and give up. Perhaps it is similar to when we have not tuned into a certain radio station or we have not yet updated a certain software program. It doesn't mean that it's not available to us; it's just that we made another choice or we simply were not even aware that it was available. Once we experience His love and peace, there is no turning back. It's the beginning of an amazing relationship where faith and love always continues to grow and blossom. Faith is the currency in heaven like money is the currency on earth.

And without faith it is impossible to please God, because anyone who comes to him must believe that he exists and that he rewards those who earnestly seek him. Hebrews 11:6 (NIV). Why is it that without faith, it is impossible to please God? It's because He wants the best for us, and if we don't' have faith, the results will not be what He wants for us. We empower what we believe. We can't manipulate energy and frequency. We will always get to choose what we empower. **The tongue has the power of life and death, and those who love it will eat its fruit. Proverbs 18:21 (NIV).**

Sin leads to death. In Him is life. Outside of Him [love]...is sin and death. Could a loving Father have made it so easy for us? **And he said: "Truly I tell you, unless you change and become like little children, you will never enter the kingdom of heaven. Matthew 18:3 (NIV).** In the Kingdom, there is no sickness, and there is no death.

We have perhaps overcomplicated things...until now! When we are in the realm of love, our words, thoughts, and actions are loving. Our bodies are at ease. So, the deeper we go into love - the closer we will be to more answers and to all the gifts that He's already provided for us to receive, for an amazing long life.

Never again will there be in it an infant who lives but a few days, or an old man who does not live out his years; the one who dies at a hundred will be thought a mere child; the one who fails to reach a hundred will be considered accursed. Isaiah 65:20 (NIV).

The good news today is that we are realizing that we have such a loving Father and there is so much more. We are never to think and believe that we are victims or orphans. We are royalty with such a huge inheritance.

A child of the King is free to dream with no limits

>…an orphan can only see by their own limitations.

A child of the King knows they are loved and belong to their Father

>…an orphan struggles to fit in and always feels left out.

A child of the King walks in their Father's authority

>…an orphan operates in his own limited authority.

A child of the King receives comfort from their Father

>…an orphan seeks comfort from things and substitutes.

A child of the King believes in life and blessings

>…an orphan believes solely in what they see.

A child of the King believes in extended long life

>…an orphan believes in his *own ability* to stay alive as long as he can.

The good news is that you always have access to the Father [love]. You can always speak and listen to Him in your heart. God [love] will always guide you into the truth for your highest good. It's all good news! You have to seek for yourself and you will find Him.

On our journey, there will be Satan who will try to steal, kill, and destroy our lives. It's important for us to know the truth, so that we don't fall prey to his lies. It's also important to expose what he tries to do and to not just ignore it, thinking it will just go away. We can't just keep it hidden in the dark we must face it and get rid of it.

A different way of approaching this would be to say that there are forces of negative energy and negative frequency in our lives that will come in various forms. For example, they can manifest when we agree with thoughts from our past that make us feel guilty or ashamed. Or, when we take offense, overeat, or drink too much. It can also come in other forms through other addictions like gambling and pornography. Or, by worrying and fearing about things such as lack, sickness, and death. Those are just a few examples of how the thief comes to kill, steal, and to destroy the abundant life that God [love] already has paid for us to have and enjoy. If you'll notice, these are all separate from love, and they all lead to disease in our body, which eventually leads to death. The good news is that we are now starting to see and to know the truth, and the truth is setting us free from the lies that have kept us in defeat.

You make known to me the path of life; you will fill me with joy in your presence, with eternal pleasures at your right hand. Psalm 16:11 (NIV). There are so many levels of His truth. The deeper we go, the deeper our level of joy and victory will be in our lives. Joy doesn't just come and go, it's always available. It is a fruit of the Spirit of love. It's when we tap into the frequency of love that we find true joy. God is love.

Therefore, I urge you, brothers and sisters, because of God's mercy, to offer your bodies as a living sacrifice, holy and pleasing to God—this is your true and proper worship. Do not conform to the pattern of this world, but be transformed by the renewing of your mind. Then you can test and approve what God's will is—his good, pleasing and perfect will. Romans 12:1-2 (NIV).

He tells us to offer our bodies as living sacrifices. Basically, giving up living just by how we feel, see, hear, touch, and smell (our five senses) and going deeper by living in the spirit. We have a spiritual, mental, and physical self and our spirit (one with love) is what should be dictating or directing our flesh (physical) not our flesh directing our spirit.

The mind governed by the flesh is death, but the mind governed by the Spirit is life and peace. Romans 8:6 (NIV).

Being one with God [love] is where all wisdom, peace, and joy is. It is when we live from love that we have control over our flesh. ***"Your kingdom come, your will be done, on earth as it is in heaven." Matthew 6:10 (NIV).*** We should be bringing heaven here on earth and not trying to bring earth to heaven. ***Praise be to the God and Father of our Lord Jesus Christ, who has blessed us in the heavenly realms with every spiritual blessing in Christ. Ephesians 1:3 (NIV).*** We have already been blessed with all spiritual blessings. Most of what we pray for, we already have. He's already provided all that we need, and He's given us the authority here on earth. It's been said, that our prayers are often anchored in unbelief because we pray for what we've already been given.

God [love] also tells us not to conform to the patterns of the world. What are some of those patterns of the world in your life? Here are some examples.

- As soon as we feel sick, we immediately call a doctor or search online for the solutions, versus...first seeking what God's Word says about it.

- As soon as we reach a certain age (it's different for everyone) we come in agreement that we will die soon, versus...seeking what the truth is in His Word.

- When we are children, we start school so that one day, we can get a good job. Then many years later, we get a job, and we work hard and put work first - so that we can have a good retirement. Then, once we retire, we end up spending most of our savings on health issues because we were always under so much stress, and we were so busy. We didn't have much time to search for His [love] truth. Instead, we chose to conform to the patterns of the world, versus...co-laboring with love [God] throughout our lives and not ignoring what He had for us throughout our journey, which always was (and always will be) the abundant life, (by faith) of peace, healing, joy, abundance, long life, etc. This would have been superior and so much more satisfying and fulfilling.

- We continuously worry, fear, and try to control and figure everything out on our own, versus...trusting God [love].

- We live by seeing and then believing, versus...believing and then seeing, which is faith.

- We believe that sickness, suffering, and death is just our destiny, versus...seeking what God's truth is on the matter.

So, we are told not to conform to the patterns of the world but to be transformed (to the higher truth) by the renewing of our mind—living life and co-laboring with love [God]. This includes seeing and listening to what He is saying about our situations. What? How do you listen to love [God]? One answer is, *it's the same way you listen to worry and fear.* You just need to change the frequency channel to love.

Love's [God] voice is always the one that will comfort you. It will always be peaceful and loving. There are times when a good parent will also tell their children something that they don't want to hear, but they will know that it's meant with a good heart for their own good. So, what He tells you, or what He puts on your heart, can sometimes be hard to do - like forgiving. But you will know the difference between His loving promptings and the promptings from the evil one. Once we let go and let love [God], our whole life changes. Let's face it, we either let go and let God, or we don't let go and we let Satan. Our spiritual self is who we are, whether we acknowledge it or not. We get to decide which path (pattern) we take. As we have previously mentioned, the wages of sin is death. We know that sin is the big culprit for death. **Now, faith is confidence in what we hope for and assurance about what we do not see. Hebrews 11:1 (NIV).**

The opposite of having faith is be not being sure of what we hope for and not being certain of what we don't see. That is sin which leads to death and it's also living in the flesh. **For if you live according to the flesh, you will die; but if by the Spirit you put to death the misdeeds of the body, you will live. Romans 8:13 (NIV).**

Everything that does not come from faith is sin. Romans 14:23b (NIV).

We seem to not have faith when we can't see something that we are hoping for, or when we can't figure it out with our human minds - so we doubt and dismiss it. However, Jesus *told us we would do what He has done and even greater things.* **Very truly I tell you, whoever believes in me will do the works I have been doing, and they will do even greater things than these, because I am going to the Father. John 14:12 (NIV).** What did He do? For the subject of this book, He always defeated death. When someone asked Him to bring someone that had died back to life, He always said, "Yes." He never gave any power to death. He said they were sleeping. He never attended a funeral. He was never a friend with death and He never will be, and neither should we. One of His Disciples was a doctor and He never told him to give anyone a bad report.

Let's look at the following Scripture in Luke: **Soon afterward, Jesus went to a town called Nain, and his disciples and a large crowd went along with him. As he approached the town gate, a dead person was being carried out—the only son of his mother, and she was a widow. And a large crowd from the town was** with her. When the Lord saw her, his heart went out to her and he said, "Don't cry." Then he went up and touched the bier they were carrying him on, and the bearers stood still. He said, "Young man, I say to you, get up!" The dead man sat up and began to talk, and Jesus gave him back to his mother. They were all filled with awe and praised God. Luke 7:11-15 (NIV).

"While Jesus was still speaking, someone came from the house of Jairus, the synagogue leader. "Your daughter is dead," he said. "Don't bother the teacher anymore."

Hearing this, Jesus said to Jairus, "Don't be afraid; just believe, and she will be healed."

When he arrived at the house of Jairus, he did not let anyone go in with him except Peter, John and James, and the child's father and mother. Meanwhile, all the people were wailing and mourning for her. "Stop wailing," Jesus said. "She is not dead but asleep."

They laughed at him, knowing that she was dead. But he took her by the hand and said, "My child, get up!" Her spirit returned, and at once she stood up. Then Jesus told them to give her something to eat. Her parents were astonished, but he ordered them not to tell anyone what had happened. Luke 8:41-56 (NIV).

Then Jesus said, "Did I not tell you that if you believe, you will see the glory of God?" So, they took away the stone. Then Jesus looked up and said, "Father, I thank you that you have heard me. I knew that you always hear me, but I said this for the benefit of the people standing here, that they may believe that you sent me." When he had said this, Jesus called in a loud voice, "Lazarus, come out!" The dead man came out, his hands and feet wrapped with strips of linen, and a cloth around

his face. Jesus said to them, "Take off the grave clothes and let him go." John 11:40-44 (NIV).

When you read these encounters from 'death to life,' what do you sense in your spirit? When you let go of the patterns of the world regarding death, what do you now see? Do you see a Father who loves you so much and wants the very best for you? Are you seeing that perhaps death really is not a part of love? If, the Kingdom of God lives in us and nothing is impossible for those that believe; do you think that perhaps there is more to just living to be a certain age, and then making an agreement with the spirit of death?

What if we turned on the TV for the next several days and saw news segments like the following examples:

- Dr. Chauncey, Cardiologist in Florida, being interviewed about the book he wrote that included the testimony about one of his patients (age 53) that had died of a massive heart attack. And about 40 minutes later, the Holy Spirit put on his heart to pray for him to come back to life. A nurse was preparing the body according to the protocol to get it ready for the morgue and the family, and here comes Dr. Chauncey telling her he will pray for the dead man. Of course, his five senses were not cheering him on...but his spirit was. So, he prayed for him, and they shocked him one more time and the patient came back to life...the nurse screamed!

- What if they interviewed Annalise Janse Van Rensburg in Africa? Her husband had a huge ministry where thousands were healed. He was personally raised from the dead numerous times.

- What if they had a clip of Tyler G. Johnson, who has a ministry that has affected thousands of people all over the world with his teachings plus many recorded cases of people being raised from the dead? One being when his five-year-old son prayed on the phone for the father of one of his good friends, who was later brought back to life. Several years later, Tyler was doing a conference in a city on the west coast, and this man came up to him and shook his hand and gave him the biggest hug. Tyler was somewhat taken aback because this hug was so strong, and the man was so emotional. He then found out that this was the man that his son had prayed for that had been resurrected. The man then went to his truck and returned with a little wooden bench he had made. It had special words carved on it and he gave it to Tyler to give to his son.

- What if they interviewed David Hogan from Freedom Ministries? Their ministry has witnessed over 400 people coming back from death to life.

- What if they included a segment on Reinhard Bonke's story when he was in Africa years ago? He was scheduled to preach at a local church where they brought a dead man who had been embalmed, but his wife had totally refused to accept death. They put him in the basement of that church when Reinhard preached, and he came back to life. They have all the medical records to prove it.

- What if they interviewed leaders at Bethel Church in Redding, California, where there are thousands of testimonies (medically confirmed) of people being healed of terminal illnesses?

If we would see these types of testimonies daily on the news, sooner than later, it would become more real to us. We would easily form patterns to believe. The power of the testimony cannot be overstated, it is always so powerful. We are so much more than what we can ever think or imagine. No wonder in God's Word, He tells us to just believe.

It's perhaps similar to the Olympics. We would have never

thought back in the 90's that someone would run the 100m at 9.58 seconds, or the 200m at 19.19 seconds. But Usain Bolt, also known as Lightning Bolt, did it. So now, our minds have been reprogrammed to believe and think that we can do it even faster. We receive what we believe. **For as he thinks in his heart, so is he. Proverbs 23:7 (KJV).**

How big is your God? Do you really believe what He says? Do you believe that He loves you so much and that He really defeated death for you? You get to choose!

The good news is that whatever choice you make, He doesn't love you any less or any more. He loves you one hundred percent – one hundred percent of the time!

As for you, the anointing you received from him remains in you, and you do not need anyone to teach you. But as his anointing teaches you about all things and as that anointing is real, not counterfeit—just as it has taught you, remain in him. 1 John 2:27 (NIV).

Keep seeking, and you will find the truth. Be ready for your answers to come in many different ways. Here is an example from a true story:

It was two years ago, in February Abby was getting ready to decorate her home for St. Valentine's day. But she still had several large bright red poinsettia plants from Christmas. She couldn't transplant them outside in the cold snowy weather. She knew that she would have to throw them out. She was sad because she felt that she was taking something that was alive and killing it.

As she was throwing them out in the big bin outside by her garage door, she felt the Holy Spirit put on her heart that it was okay...and that nothing ever dies. What? She could feel the power of those words. She took some time to immediately 'pause and ponder'. For the first time, she could see and understand that nothing ever dies. In this case the flowers would just change to another form of matter. The revelation that she received that day started her lifetime search for more of what that all meant. She recognizes that there is so much more to those three words that God whispered in her ear that day, "Nothing ever dies."

Wow!

Nothing ever dies

He is before all things, and in him all things hold together. Colossians 1:17 (NIV).

He is life and there is no death in Him. He is abundant life and He lives in us. Do you see? Do you believe?

Jesus said to her, "I am the resurrection and the life. The one who believes in me will live, even though they die.

And whoever lives by believing in me will never die. Do you believe this?" John 11:25-26 (NIV).

TWO

We Are As He Is...On Earth Today

Everything in life takes after its source. Animals bring forth after their kind. Plants look like the stem they budded from, and children also take after their parents. As expressed in Genesis, God's original intention was to make man in His image and after His likeness. *So, God created mankind in his own image, in the image of God, he created them; male and female, he created them. Genesis 1:27 (NIV).*

Even after sin came and man sought his selfish desire, the ultimate purpose of salvation and redemption was to return man to his original nature - which is to be like God. We all agree that children take after their parents. And since we are children of God, we take after our heavenly Father.

The Bible says in *Ephesians 4:11-13 (KJV), And he gave some, apostles; and some, prophets; and some, evangelists; and some, pastors and teachers; for the perfecting of the saints, for the work of the ministry, for the edifying of the body of Christ: Till we all come in the unity of the faith, and of the knowledge of the Son of God, unto a perfect man, unto the measure of the stature of the fullness of Christ.* So, the whole pursuit of the body of Christ is to raise saints that are like Christ.

In this chapter, we will focus on this Scripture, *As He is, so are we in this world. 1 John 4:17 (NKJV).*

First, I would like to mention that this chapter was influenced by a great man of God, whose name is, Chris Blackeby. He is the founder of, *As He is Ministries*.

God has used some of Chris' teachings to bring some amazing revelation and transformation in my life. Specifically, I have listened to two of his teachings, repeatedly. So much so, that if those teachings were on the old cassette tapes, I would have worn them all out by now.

Chris has graciously permitted me to include several of his teaching points in this chapter to bless you. The interpretation is based on my understanding and level of revelation. I am so grateful for his kindness.

As believers, we need to be transformed by the renewing of our minds. And to recognize and understand more than ever, who we are, and what our inheritance really is, in Christ.

> **As HE is**
> **so WE are**
> **in this**
> **WORLD**
>
> **1 John 4:17 (NKJV)**

Note the astounding statement at the end of verse 17- **As He is (in heaven), so are we (here on earth).** In other words, just as He is in heaven representing us before the Father, He has positioned us strategically on the earth to represent Him.

We are Him to this earth because we are Him. We are one, as much as He and the Father are one. *I in them and you in me-so that they may be brought to complete unity. Then the world will know that you sent me and have loved them even as you have loved me. John 17:23 (NIV).*

Jesus said, "I am the Vine; you are the branches. The one who remains in Me and I in him bears much fruit, for (otherwise) apart from Me [that is, cut off from vital union with me] you can do nothing." John15:5 (AMP). The oneness in the Trinity is the same oneness we have with Him, and it's the same oneness we have among ourselves. So, we have to see ourselves as one, in like-manner. It's similar to when we look at an egg. The egg, in this example, represents God.

When people look at us, they see the Trinity as well, because we are one. Separation is always just an illusion. *For in him, we live and move and have our being. Acts 17:28 (NIV).*

For I am sure that neither death nor life, nor angels nor rulers, nor things present nor things to come, nor powers, nor height nor depth, nor anything else in all creation, will be able to separate us from the love of God. Romans 8:38-39 (ESV). Even though He is always with us, when we choose to sin, the thought of condemnation makes us turn our minds and hearts away from Him.

But your iniquities have made a separation between you and your God, and your sins have hidden his face from you so that he does not hear. Isaiah 59:2 (ESV).

When we sin, we open up the door and lower the edge for the enemy to creep in, and this act drifts us away from the love frequency, and then we start to vibrate at a lower frequency, which attracts chaos, destruction, and death.

Usually, when we are asked, "Where did sin, sickness, and death originate from?" Most of us would say, "From Adam and Eve in the Garden of Eden." But, if you read the account of Genesis, it does not say:

- "Did God say, You will surely sin?"
- "Did God say, You will surely be sick?"

Let's take a quick look at that verse. **The woman said to the serpent, "We may eat fruit from the trees in the garden, but God did say, 'You must not eat fruit from the tree that is in the middle of the garden, and you must not touch it, or you will die.'" Genesis 3:2-3 (NIV).**

> # You will not *certainly* DIE the serpent said *to the* woman
>
> **Genesis 3:4 (NIV)**

"You will not certainly die," the serpent said to the woman. Genesis 3:4 (NIV). This statement clearly illustrates that the real source of sin and death originated from the deception of the devil (the deceiver). Deception is one of the wiles of Satan to gain access into our lives.

Oh! I wish everyone could understand this truth and walk free from the enemy's deception and lies.

The root of DEATH is DECEPTION

Deception is what brought about death; it's always been the enemy. It is the root of all sin, sickness, poverty, depression, etc. The good news is that Jesus is the truth, and He has already defeated death. It is now our great privilege to stand in the light of that truth. He broke the power of death and illuminated the way to life and immortality through the 'Good News.' **So, Jesus said to the Jews who had believed him, "If you abide in my Word, you are truly my disciples, and you will know the truth, and the truth will set you free." John 8:31-32 (ESV).**

Pause for a moment … and think about what the world would look like if no one was deceived. Would it look like heaven on earth? Perhaps, those areas in our lives that we are not experiencing the reality of heaven – we are believing a lie. We have been under deceptions of all kinds.

The Bible says, **However, no one can believe unless they hear the Word of God. How, then, can they call on the one they have not believed in? And how can they believe in the one of whom they have not heard? And how can they hear without someone preaching to them? Romans 10:14 (NIV).** In other words, when we hear the preaching of God's Word, faith comes alive in us, and the hold of deception, sin, and death is loosed. **Whoever believes in Him shall not perish but have everlasting life. John 3:16 (NIV).**

The reality of this truth is that even non-Christians are beginning to align with this revelation. For instance, companies like Google and Amazon are all going hard after long life and immortality because biologically, there is no reason we can't defy death.

So, the big question is, 'Why are people still dying'? The short and direct response is that it's a law. God has given us dominion on the earth. Our agreement with the enemy's deception and lies opens the door to death, which is what empowers his grip into our lives. It's actually living outside the frequency of God's love.

Did you notice the Bible says that Enoch walked with God? *Walked*, meaning intertwined with Him. Enoch never died because he was continuously in the frequency of His love. **Enoch walked faithfully with God, then he was no more, because God took him away. Genesis 5:24. (NIV).**

This reminds me of an awesome testimony from Milly Bennitt from Cabin Academy, who spoke about the day when she was with her Mom doing dishes, and she became so caught up in the frequency of the Holy Spirit, her body started disappearing. Her Mom witnessed it, and she freaked out.

It happened another time when she was working on a temporary assignment in a corporate setting. Again, she got so intertwined with the frequency of His love (God), that she had to stand up and walk around, so that she could function. So, she went to another floor to visit a co-worker. When he saw her (with part of her body looking translucent) he equally freaked out, and the experience made him request for new eyeglasses.

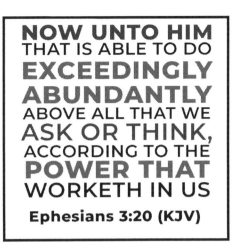

These types of testimonies are just the beginning of so much more.

As previously mentioned, the fall in the Garden of Eden is clearly about deception, leading to death (not about sin, per say). We are to understand that Jesus abolished death once and for all.

God's original plan for Adam and Eve was constant communication and fellowship with Him. Death was never intended to be a part of it.

The thief comes only to steal and kill and destroy; I have come that they may have life and have it to the full. John 10:10 (NIV). Jesus came and destroyed death's agenda. God's original plan for Adam and Eve is still in force with us today, which is everlasting life. **On earth, as it is in heaven. Matthew 6:10 (NIV).** Hallelujah! This is such good news.

However, it takes the power of the Holy Spirit to pull down the blinders (deception) in our minds about death. But once that transformation begins, we will suddenly start to see and understand "life and immortality" at a new level. For instance, Scriptures like the following, will start to come alive in our spirit.

In the way of righteousness, there is life; along that path is immortality. Proverbs 12:28 (NIV).

For the perishable must clothe itself with the imperishable, and the mortal with immortality. When the perishable has been clothed with the imperishable and the mortal with immortality, then the saying that is written will come true: "Death has been swallowed up in victory." 1 Corinthians 15:53-54 (NIV).

But it has now been revealed through the appearing of our Savior, Christ Jesus, who has destroyed death and has brought life and immortality to light through the gospel. 2 Timothy 1:10 (NIV).

To those who by persistence in doing good seek glory, honor and immortality, he will give eternal life. Romans 2:7 (NIV).

Look at **John 3:16 (NIV)** closely. *For God so loved the world, that he gave his one and only Son, that whoever believes in him shall not perish but have eternal life.* This Scripture does not use the term "immortality" when it speaks of "everlasting life," but it refers to bodily immortality. Usually, when the Bible speaks of "life," it often refers to bodily immortality, not conscious of the spiritual form but the body.

As believers, we are presented with two options;

Option One:

Jesus said to her, "I am the resurrection and the life. The one who believes in me will live, even though they die." John 11:25 (NIV).

Option Two:

"And whoever lives by believing in me will never die." Do you believe this? John 11:26 (NIV).

In the *first option*, Jesus says, "I am the resurrection, and I am the life, if you believe in Me, you will live, even though you die." Here there is physical death, and then we get to be in heaven. This is the prominent belief system that we've had as a culture.

However, in the *second option,* He says, "You can believe in me and *never* die." It's so clear here. Do you see?

Immortality, is all throughout the Gospels, including the Old Testament. Once you open your heart to it, everything written in the Word starts to come alive at a new level.

That's why the spirit said, "If you hear God's voice today, don't be stubborn as in the past when you turned against God." Hebrews 3:15 (ERV). We are to make our hearts receptive to the new light from His Word. We can't just keep ignoring and deleting what He is showing us, because we can't figure it all out.

Let's examine some Biblical heroes of faith who demonstrated the reality of immortality, while they were physically on the earth. They simply demonstrated that we are 'as He is', on the earth.

Join me as we zoom in on the Apostle Paul.

Paul was immortal, and he demonstrated that we have a choice, whether to be alive or to die. The truth of immortality engulfed him such that he began to negotiate either to stay alive or to die. Eventually, he laid his life willingly, after several failed attempts to be killed.

Paul tells us that he was stoned. Understand that "stoned" meant to be executed. Back then, stoning was always intended to kill the individual. (Example: Stephen in Act 7:59) but Paul was still alive.

Jews came from Antioch and Iconium and having persuaded the crowds, they stoned Paul and dragged him out of the city, supposing that he was dead. But when the disciples gathered about him, he rose up and entered the city. Acts 14:19 – 20a (ESV).

After he was stoned, he picked himself up again and continued preaching in the next city. He had also been shipwrecked, flogged, and bitten by a snake. Yet, he didn't pray about the unfair treatment; neither did he make declarations against the situation. Rather, he shook it off because he had no thought of death in his heart.

Paul gathered a pile of brushwood and, as he put it on the fire, a

viper, driven out by the heat, fastened itself on his hand. When the islanders saw the snake hanging from his hand, they said to each other, "This man must be a murderer; for though he escaped from the sea, the goddess Justice has not allowed him to live." But Paul shook the snake off into the fire and suffered no ill effects. Acts 28:3-5 (NIV).

Also, Jesus never recognized death. He described it as mere sleeping. He didn't even like to mention the word "death." Even when He talked about His own death, He referred to it as going to be with the Father. **You heard me say, 'I am going away, and I am coming back to you.' If you loved me, you would be glad that I am going to the Father, for the Father is greater than I. John 14:28 (NIV).**

Also, when He was telling the disciples about His death and resurrection in **John 2:19 (NIV), He said, "Destroy this temple, and I will raise it again in three days."**

He didn't use the term 'death'. It was always an enemy. He never made friends with it. He never let it intimidate Him. Neither, did He ever give death any power.

Meanwhile, all the people were wailing and mourning for her. "Stop wailing," Jesus said. "She is not dead but asleep." Luke 8:52 (NIV).

What about John, the beloved? Did he die? We don't know if he gave up his life at any time. We know that Enoch never experienced physical death. It's also interesting how Elijah and Moses took up their bodies again. **After he became the father of Methuselah, Enoch walked faithfully with God for 300 years and had other sons and daughters. Altogether, Enoch lived a total of 365 years. Enoch walked faithfully with God; then he was no more, because God took him away. Genesis 5:22-24 (NIV).**

As they were walking along and talking together, suddenly a chariot of fire and horses of fire appeared and separated the two of them,

and Elijah went up to heaven in a whirlwind. 2 Kings 2:11 (NIV).

In Jude 9, it refers to the story in which the archangel Michael disputes with the devil about the body of Moses. Why? Because he took it up again and appeared to Jesus on the Mount of Transfiguration, and Elijah could appear too, because he never left his body behind.

> **Jesus NEVER gave any power to Death**
>
> **And neither should we**

So, it's important never to give power or make any agreement with death... ever!

Jesus came to destroy death at such a high cost, to give us abundant life. His death is your victory! He is your everything but He is never your death.

> **Jesus' Death Is Our Victory**

If we have died with Christ, we believe that we will also live with him. We know that Christ, being raised from the dead, will never die again;

death no longer has dominion over him. For the death he died to sin, once for all, but the life he lives, he lives to God. In the same way, count yourselves dead to sin but alive to God in Christ Jesus. So you also must consider yourselves dead to sin and alive to God in Christ Jesus. Therefore, do not let sin reign in your mortal body so that you obey its evil desires. Romans 6:10-12 (NIV).

Now, that we are starting to see the truth regarding immortality - let's get ready for a huge upgrade in our lives. Get ready for an increase in your understanding of His love to a whole new level.

We must continue to seek and believe in the truth of His Word; so that our children and our children's children and the next generations will never have to live in deception, destruction, and death.

When I see science achieving giant strides in this area of super long life and immortality, I know that the children of God should already be way ahead of any of those discoveries. God, who is in us, knows the end from the beginning.

Even if immortality wasn't in His Word, it would make no sense for a loving Father to ever murder his children with sickness, pain, and death. Don't you agree?

God is LOVE - He never actually created us to die

GOD IS THE PERFECT FATHER

He does NOT kill His children

God made it so easy for us. He told us in His Word that He has defeated death. We just need to believe.

The following are some thought-provoking questions. Especially when we are told that we are as He is on this earth. **As He is, so are we in this world. 1 John 4:17 (NKJV).** Let's now look at some thought provoking questions.

Thought Provoking Question #1

What would we do if we saw Jesus crying because a child died, and He didn't believe in resurrection?

Thought Provoking Question #2

What would we do if we saw Jesus depending on certain foods to keep him alive and healthy?

Thought Provoking Question #3

What would we do if we heard Jesus saying, "I'm getting old, and I can't do that anymore?"

Thought Provoking Queston #4

What would we do if we saw Jesus engulfed with worry and fear about death?

We need to walk in His victory. Otherwise, we are nullifying what He did on the cross for each one of us. That can be the most sobering thought ever!

We need to stop the nonsense. The truth remains: **As He is, so are we in this world. 1 John 4:17 (NKJV).**

Before sin entered the Garden of Eden, it was paradise. It was heaven on earth. However, when death entered, it became a shadow of itself. The impact of death affected the level of glory on the whole earth, which included animals, flowers, food, nature, etc. Otherwise, we would still have glorified animals, trees, etc. Can you imagine a glorified lion walking around? Of course, it has not been happening because they have all been subject to death.

We know that the whole creation has been groaning as in the pains of

childbirth right up to the present time. Not only so, but we ourselves, who have the first fruits of the Spirit, groan inwardly as we wait eagerly for our adoption to sonship, the redemption of our bodies. For in this hope we were saved. But hope that is seen is no hope at all. Who hopes for what they already have? Romans 8:22-24 (NIV).

So, we must let go of death's mental structures and come into our inheritance in all areas. Because the Scripture says; ***For as he thinketh in his heart, so is he. Proverbs 23:7 (KJV).***

On earth, as it is in heaven. Matthew 6:10b (NIV). Animals, nature, and even food do not die in heaven; it's all glory. I have personally seen glimpses of heaven. In my experience, the glory looked like the most beautiful pixie dust, especially when I saw it all over the live flowers. They were so alive and vibrant. I think that's why I love cartoons. It brings me back to what is possible and true by seeing it in my imagination without any limitations. Guess what? Food is also alive, and it doesn't ever die. It looks similar to the flowers. They are all so beautiful. In fact, there are no words to describe the splendor in heaven. By the way, animals don't die either.

There is zero death in heaven, and so should there also be zero death in your life. Say, after me, "From now on, it's zero death around me, and in me."

Let's finish this chapter with this verse.

Not only so, but we ourselves, who have the firstfruits of the Spirit, groan inwardly as we wait eagerly for our adoption to sonship, the redemption of our bodies. Romans 8:23 (NIV).

So, are we adopted?

As we wait eagerly for our adoption to sonship, the redemption of our bodies. Romans 8:23b (NIV).

The answer is 'yes.'

What does that really mean?

The redemption of our bodies - we are redeemed from the decaying of our bodies.

What's the redemption, and what's the hope that we are waiting for?

This adoption means that our bodies were already redeemed.

That is heaven coming to earth. As we change (because the earth was made from heaven) the earth changes. Also, as we glorify, we can give away what we have.

But if we don't believe that we can be glorified, we won't manifest it. If you believe in miracles, then you can give it away. You must first believe. How about believing in the redemption of your bodies? So, that is the hope of our adoption, the redemption of our bodies.

We have the Spirit, and we are a new creation. We get to be raised in heavenly places, all without dying - physically. He's done so much for us...our inheritance is huge!

Overhearing what they said, Jesus told him, "Don't be afraid; just believe."

Do you believe?

By faith, we can lay hold of this eternal truth and finally see the manifestation of our victory over death. We've had the victory all along...deception is what's been keeping us from receiving it. Do you believe?

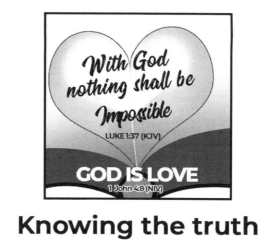

Knowing the truth is a life-changer.

THREE

Hard Questions — Easy Answers

Life sometimes feels like a pile of unanswered questions, especially as it pertains to God's love towards us. At every junction, we may face challenges and situations that make us question His love. We find ourselves thinking, "Does He really love me? Does He care about me?"

Furthermore, when we read the Old Testament, it is even more confusing because God seems like a tyrannous dictator. Especially, when it appears that He's the one that issues instructions to kill and annihilate an entire nation.

Imagine living for a long time and one day discovering that you have been completely deceived? Imagine finding out that you had lived your entire life believing lies, which created false anchors for destructive belief systems throughout your entire existence on the earth?

Only to find out that we *all* had been living one *big* lie. And most importantly, that the truth had simply remained dormant. It's like we had never been awakened to it. Or, we simply had never been set free, to be able to see it.

Perhaps the purpose of this book is for the Holy Spirit to nudge you and to provoke you into seeing that there might be more to what you have been believing. We must see that our God is loving and sovereign, and we must seek Him for the answers.

> **ASK...**
> *And it will be given to you*
>
> **SEEK...**
> *And you will find*
>
> **KNOCK...**
> *And the door will be opened to you*
>
> **Matthew 7:7 (NIV)**

We need to expose the lies so that old patterns of thinking can be broken off. Get ready for a fun and encouraging time in this chapter. There is no way that anyone can tap into long life, if the foundation of His truth is not established as a strong foundation.

Then you will know the truth, and the truth will set you free. John 8:32 (NIV).

One person whose teachings on this subject has influenced and transformed my life is an amazing man of God, named Tyler G Johnson, from One Glance Ministries. I view him as an amazing forerunner on the subject of *God's love and immortality*. The remarkable insights and revelations that I've received from his teachings inspired me to write this chapter. I believe that you will be blessed as I share some "mind-boggling" truths with you.

It started back in 2010, when Reinhard Bonke came to our city to minister during a 'breakfast impartation service.' I was privileged to be at the planning meeting in preparation for the big event. In that season of my life, I had also been hosting different speakers (to speak in our city) those that God highlighted for me to invite. Once they accepted the invitation, I would reserve conference rooms in friendly hotels, even without an inkling of the number of people that were going to show up for the meetings.

Each time I received such divine instruction, I shared it with my good friends, Sonia and Doug. Without any hesitation, they always joined hands with me, to plan for the conferences.

We weren't Pastors nor did we have any formal titles. But we were obedient to God's calling by inviting these men and women of God, who opened up new dimensions of His truth. They shared profound revelations that were rarely talked about in most churches.

At Reinhard's planning meeting, someone recommended that I invite Tyler to be one of our speakers. They also informed me that he prayed for people (including children) to be raised from the dead—some on their deathbed and others that had just passed on.

When I heard about it, I freaked out, and I certainly wasn't in favor of extending such an invitation. My mind immediately said, "No!" However, I remember that my spirit didn't oppose; neither was it offended.

Eventually, we invited Tyler, and without any doubt, he was such a unique gift from God. During his meetings, so many people's lives were impacted in such powerful ways. He has such a deep revelation of God's Word. He teaches about God's love with an exceptional depth of insight. He often refers to immortality as simply being a by-product of God's love.

Although His teachings can make your brain tilt, the revelation that he imparts also makes your spirit rejoice. **Therefore, I urge you, brothers and sisters, because of God's mercy, to offer your bodies as a living sacrifice, holy and pleasing to God—this is your true and proper worship. Do not conform to this world's pattern, but be transformed by the renewing of your mind. Then you will be able to test and approve what God's will is - his good, pleasing, and perfect will. Romans 12:1-2 (NIV).**

Tyler and I have become good friends, he is like a son. I am forever grateful for the sacrifices that his wonderful wife Christine (and his family) have made, which has enabled him to preach and teach, as a forerunner, on the subject of "immortality" and so much more.

I will share, some of what we spoke about recently in this chapter. I've added my own comments and revelations as well. I pray that the Holy Spirit will further minister the truth to you. **For the Word of God is alive and active, sharper than any double-edged sword, it penetrates even to dividing soul and spirit, joints and marrow; it judges the thoughts and attitudes of the heart. Hebrews 4:12 (NIV).**

TYLER'S GRINDING SEASON

Over fifteen years ago, Tyler's Dad (who was one of his best friends) suddenly died in his arms while they were both working at a job site.

Indeed, a loved one's death is one of the most challenging thing anyone can ever imagine. During and after the shock and trauma, Tyler had a choice to make. Was he going to get angry at God and question His love? Or, was he going to seek-out the deeper truth about this heart-wrenching (very unfair) event in his life? And was he going to find out the 'why' while keeping an open mind, free of offense?

Eventually, Tyler decided to find answers to the many "hard questions" bowling in his mind. The more he studied the Scriptures, especially the Book of Solomon, the deeper he saw God's love.

One day, he stumbled on the truth that showed him that there is absolutely no death in God. Neither was God a murderer, nor was He bipolar. Through this revelation, Tyler saw and experienced (at a new level) how God's love for all of us is so unique, incomparable and boundless. He saw how God is love. This truth became a huge reality in his life.

Now years later, when he teaches about immortality (all these are my personal observations), he often simplifies it all by saying, "God is good, and the enemy is bad. Life is good because it's from God. Death is bad because it's from the enemy."

God never has any part in death. *The thief does not come except to steal, to kill, and to destroy. But Jesus came to give us life and that in abundance. John 10:10 (NKJV).*

Through Tyler's personal experience and revelation concerning God's Word, he now spends time daily - encouraging, ministering, and praying for those who have lost loved ones. He also travels internationally and teaches God's truth. As a result, his ministry has witnessed many resurrections, all to the glory of God. The impartation when he ministers continues to always be life-changing.

Interestingly, one of Tyler's deepest prayer is that one day, we will all come into agreement with God's Word and believe that He's already defeated death. Once we reach that point, we won't even have to raise people from the dead!

Perhaps, that is why the Bible refers to raising the dead as elementary. We are to move beyond what is considered just elementary. Look at this Scripture! Wow!

Therefore, let us move beyond the elementary teachings about Christ and be taken forward to maturity, not laying again the foundation of repentance from acts that lead to death, and of faith in God, instruction about cleansing rites, the laying on of hands, the resurrection of the dead, and eternal judgment. Hebrews 6:1-2 (NIV).

In other words, God expects us to move beyond just raising the dead. Instead, we are to come to the knowledge of the truth and begin to take steps that lead to the abundant life in Christ.

At this point, I will share some of the hard questions that we discussed for this chapter. The answers were filtered through the lens of my own personal revelation.

Humanity is on a journey of bringing the fullness of the Kingdom of God to the earth. There are immediate blessings available to anyone who believes that when Jesus died, He provided total forgiveness of sins, healing, and immortality. All of it, instantly becomes available to the believer. So, how many people believe in that truth? We have to believe to receive.

Perhaps that is where the journey begins, to gain insight into what the truth really is. **So then faith comes by hearing and hearing by the word of God. Romans 10:17 (NKJV).** The blood of Jesus results in everlasting life to include our physical life, in this realm, now. If we're honest, not many people believe this truth. But the good news is that the number of people who now believe, keeps growing daily, all over the world.

Since God is not for death, He sent Jesus to destroy sin and death. However, most people still suffer from sin because they haven't accepted the gift of life through Jesus. They have not yet received the greatest gift of salvation, which is eternal life (immortality).

Tapping into immortality is the same as tapping into healing. Most of us who grew up in the church were perhaps in a denomination that didn't embrace the reality of physical healing or the manifestations of God's glory. So, we ended up not experiencing any of it, because we will receive what we believe.

In the Kingdom of God, you have to believe for something before you receive it, and that's called "faith". It's a Kingdom principle and also a childlike reality, where we believe in something before we can actually see it. **Now faith is the substance of things hoped for, the evidence of things not seen. Hebrews 11:1 (KJV).**

Every reality in the Kingdom of God is accessed through faith. If people don't believe in immortality, they will not experience it here on earth.

So, it's up to the remnant that's on the earth today, the small percentage of people that believe to be faithful enough to preach the Word. People won't know the fullness of the gospel unless it's preached. How does faith come? It comes by hearing the Word. **So, then faith comes by hearing and hearing by the Word of God. Romans 10:17 (NKJV).** It comes by the preaching of the Word. **How then can they call on the one they have not believed in? And how can they believe in the one of whom they have not heard? And how can they hear without someone preaching to them? Romans 10:14 (NIV).**

For those divinely given the revelation of immortality, we don't just strive to walk in it. Although, that will be a huge part of our testimony. We will manifest this reality by being faithful to preach it at every chance we get. The Holy Spirit will always be there to guide us.

Hey! Friend, rejoice! We are currently at an exciting moment in time with humanity. I believe that we're at the very cusp, and the very beginning, of what God wants to do regarding immortality. I believe that there have been forerunners who have tried to communicate this to humanity throughout time.

The good news is there are currently more than just a few forerunners preaching and teaching it. There are people from so many live streams, with different denominational persuasions, that are all hearing the same thing from the Holy Spirit.

I came that they may have life and have it abundantly. John 10:10 (ASV).

But it has now been revealed through the appearing of our Savior Christ Jesus, who has destroyed death and has brought life and immortality to light through the gospel. 2 Timothy 1:10 (NIV).

HE ABOLISHED DEATH

2 Timothy 1:10 (KJV)

The central part of the gospel is about immortality. To leave that part out makes life confusing. It brings us to experiencing gaps in what we believe. Because we don't know how to fill the gaps with Godly revelation, we quietly withdraw back to our comfortable ideas about life, death, and all that it entails. Rather than reaching out by faith, to lay hold of the full picture of what God has done, and will do for us. He is eternal, and we're supposed to be like Him. **As He is, so are we in this world. 1 John 4:17 (KJV).**

The truth is that God doesn't want us to die. We know **the thief comes to steal, kill, and destroy. John 10:10 (NIV).** God is eternal, and He has no end. **Before the mountains were born or you brought forth the whole world, you are God from everlasting to everlasting. Psalm 90:2 (NKJV).**

We also know that God did not create humanity (from the beginning) with Adam and Eve, in an atmosphere of sin. **For the wages of sin is death, but God's gift is eternal life in Christ Jesus, our Lord. Romans 6:23 (NIV).**

God is LOVE - He never actually created us to die

They were originally outside the wages of sin, where there was no death. It's not until we receive the gospel of immortality, through faith, that we're going to stop experiencing death. We will keep receiving what we believe. **And whatsoever is not of faith is sin. Romans 14:23b (ASV).** Life (immortality) and sin don't ever mix.

We can even 'back-up' and look at the following:

- Most people don't even believe that death comes from the enemy.

- A lot of people still believe that death is a friend of God.

- Many people believe that death is the only way to heaven.

- People see death as their Savior…not Jesus.

Moreover, none of those belief systems are Scriptural. We have been deceived, and we have believed lies.

The last enemy to be destroyed is death. 1 Corinthians 15:26 (NIV). God is not a friend of death. We need to stop believing in death more than we do God's Word. We need to stop embracing it like an old friend, rather than a foe, that we ward off. We cannot continue to ignore this truth because it's uncomfortable, or because we can't figure it all out.

We need a universal mind-shift about death. We need the mind of Christ to come unto humanity. So, people can see that the cross and the resurrection covers everything. Until that time comes…the inheritance is death.

While in Jesus, our inheritance is and always has been immortal life. ***For we know that since Christ was raised from the dead, he cannot die again; death no longer has mastery over him. Romans 6:9 (NIV). Now if we died with Christ, we believe that we will also live with him. Romans 6:8 (NIV).*** There is never any inclination of death ever being any part of Him. Do you now see this truth?

What about 'The Plagues of Egypt'? Was God angry, and did He kill people back then?

So, when it comes to the Plagues of Egypt, God warned Egypt about what the enemy would be gaining access to, if they continued in sin. We know that sin opened up an opportunity for the enemy to inflict all the plagues, including the firstborns' deaths in Egypt.

So, God would speak from heaven, and Moses would hear Egypt's warning, because sin gives the enemy a legal right to afflict. That's why our Papa in heaven doesn't want us to engage with sin. The outcome is always unpleasant. It's not, that He is first and foremost concerned about our morality. He's not the kind of parent that says, "Do this because I said so." God always has good reasons for His instructions. Which is why He instructed us to live righteous and holy; so, that His plan for our lives can come to pass. **Because it is written, Be ye holy; for I am holy. 1 Peter 1:16 (KJV).**

When we water down such divine instruction, we end up living a compromised lifestyle, and as a result, we mitigate the blessing that the Lord wants to put on us. So, God always urges us to live righteously. Not because He's some moral dictator. God is never apprehensive. Instead, even when it comes to sin, He doesn't condemn any of us. Condemnation is not His emotional response to sin. **There is therefore now no condemnation to them which are in Christ Jesus, who walk not after the flesh but after the Spirit. Romans 8:1 (KJV).**

He's keen on righteousness because He knows that it's the best plan for your life. He knows that it will benefit you. You'll get to experience the realities of prosperity, blessings, peace, joy, immortality, and fruitfulness. **For physical training is of some value, but godliness has value for all things, holding promise for both the present life and the life to come. 1 Timothy 4:8 (NIV).** Godliness holds both earthly and eternal blessings and assurances. Unknown to most people, is that the greatest pleasures in life all take place, within the context of righteousness.

So, when He commanded Egypt to let the Israelites go, it's because God had a more accurate and overarching view than the rest of us can ever fathom.

We then see that the enemy gained ground through their sin, to destroy them. Different soul-biting plagues came on the Egyptians. But despite the disaster and misfortune in that land, Satan still hardened the heart of King Pharaoh, and he didn't let them go.

We fail to remember in the events of Egypt that God loved both sides.

The Son is the radiance of God's glory and the exact representation of His nature, upholding all things by His powerful word. Hebrews 1:3 (BSB).

God is love, and He always has been. He never changed His loving and caring nature throughout the Bible. **He is the same, yesterday, today, and forever. Hebrews 13:8 (NIV).** He didn't kill people in the Old Testament and then change His mind in the New Testament by not killing anyone and even raising them from the dead. No! But that is what we've believed.

Jesus came with a superior revelation and commandment, which is to love our enemies. He flattened the playing field. He was the first human to demonstrate God's kind of love (agape) on the earth. Showing us that we need to dislodge certain mindsets. For example, *these people are for us, and those people are against us.* Jesus didn't think that way because He always embodied the nature of God. **God is love. 1 John 4:8 (NIV).**

As we continue with the event in Egypt, which exposes how God loved His enemies. We can also see, that He wasn't in agreement with what they did to the Israelites; by keeping them as slaves for hundreds of years. Yet, He didn't hate Egypt, and He didn't want destruction for them, either. So, simply put...God told Moses, that they had pushed it so far with sin, and that the enemy was now able to inflict the plagues.

But you see, that's not the way that we have understood it. Because back in the days of Moses, the revelation that *Satan was real,* had not yet dawned on humanity. Significantly, few people in the Old Testament were aware or had any revelation that the devil had a role. His job description has always has been to steal, kill, and destroy. That truth wasn't spoken until Jesus revealed it in the New Testament.

"Sin, in its apex, is when it has gained all the authority through control and manipulation, and engagement with humans. It then has a full agreement with humanity, and it has humanity agreeing with every desire of hell. That's when humanity and hell are walking in complete unity, and death becomes the reality of man." -Tyler G Johnson

The wages of sin is death. Romans 6:23 (KJV). In other words, the result of sin is always death. *And the death of man is always the fulfilment*

of Satan's mission. But Jesus came to die, to remove sin, so that the wages of sin, which is death, could be removed. Hence, keeping us alive by defeating death.

We can see that the enemy wasn't acknowledged at that time in the Old Testament, so man had no idea who Satan was.

We know it wasn't God that hardened Pharaoh's heart. What would be the purpose of that? Why would God harden his heart and then destroy the land? That doesn't make any sense. On the contrary, the enemy hardened Pharaoh's heart. But man misinterpreted it to be God because they didn't have the revelation that Jesus brought in the New Testament.

Jesus is the exact representation of the Father. **The Son is the radiance of God's glory and the exact representation of his being, sustaining all things by His powerful Word. After he had provided purification for sins, he sat down at the right hand of the Majesty in heaven. Hebrews 1:3 (NIV).**

So finally, Pharaoh released God's people from slavery in Egypt; after a supposed angel went through and killed all the firstborn of Egypt.

We need to ask ourselves; would we want to spend eternity with an angel that killed babies? Are God's angels even capable of doing that?

If Jesus comes to give life in abundance, and if the enemy comes to steal, to kill, and to destroy, then why would an angel of God partner with the devil in his job description? It doesn't make any sense. Do you agree?

So again, we have to factor in what Jesus said, *"A good tree cannot bear bad fruit, and a bad tree cannot bear good fruit. Every tree that does not bear good fruit is cut down and thrown into the fire. Thus, by their fruit, you will recognize them." Matthew 7:18-20 (NIV)*. So, if they bear the fruits of stealing, killing, and destroying, we see the type of tree they are from. Scripture also says, *And no wonder, for Satan himself masquerades as an angel of light. 2 Corinthians 11:14 (NIV).* So, the people back in those days didn't have the revelation that the devil was real. That deception is a big deal!

All they knew was that God was real. But we know that the devil was also real. We know because he showed up even in the Garden of Eden. He was referenced as a snake. We know now, because of progressive revelations of action, orchestrated by the devil. We know who he is and no one debates that truth. Back in Genesis, they just saw a snake…and it's recorded as a snake.

The word devil or Satan shows up twenty-nine times in the Old Testament. In the New Testament, it shows up over two hundred times. So, there's a fundamental lack of acknowledgement that Satan is real in the Old Testament. The Jews still believe that the devil is an angel of the Lord and that he was Lucifer. Since they've rejected Jesus, the Jews lack the important messianic revelation that Jesus is the Son of God, and that He's the exact representation of the Father.

They can admit that Satan is an angel of the Lord, but they can't accept that he's the one that comes to steal, to kill, to destroy and that God is the giver of life. Because when a man rejects Jesus, he also rejects the revelation that Jesus comes to give life, and that the devil wants to steal, kill and to destroy.

The bottom line is God loves everybody, and He consistently urges everyone to seek righteousness. However, when we don't keep His Word and we don't stay away from sin, we expose our lives to the destructive acts of the devil. It's a level playing field, and Jesus came to save and to forgive everyone, if we'll receive Him. **The Lord is not slack concerning his promise, as some men count slackness; but is longsuffering toward us, not willing that any should perish, but that all should come to repentance. 2 Peter 3:9 (NKJV)**.

Immortality is simply a by-product of His deep love for us.

The short answer is, He didn't.

Humanity is in a state of progression with technology, religion, science, and so much more. Sometimes what we call progress is not always real progress. One area where we are continually learning about progress is in our walk with God.

In the Old Testament, man believed that God was a wrathful tyrant. They had no idea that an enemy was working in the background. So, whenever something terrible happened, whether it was stealing, killing, or destruction, man usually interpreted such unfortunate events as the act of God; rather than the enemy of their souls, which was the devil. Whatever you want to call him, he was the one responsible. This truth is validated from different parts of Scripture.

For example, when David numbered Israel. It was against God's instruction to number Israel, and you would expect King David - a man that trembles at the Word of God, to know better. This single act was recorded twice in the Bible.

First, in Samuel, and also in Chronicles.

The book of **2 Samuel 24:1 (CEV) says, The LORD was angry at Israel again, and he made David think it would be a good idea to count the people in Israel and Judah.** And seventy thousand people died as a result of the census.

But then when you look at **1 Chronicles 21:1 (ASV), it says, And Satan stood up against Israel, and moved David to number Israel** So, one book says, "Satan" and one book says, "God".

This reveals the fundamental issue. In man's minds, especially in the Old Testament, Satan had a field day; it's like identity theft in the Heavenly realms. That's a big deal because man blamed God for things that Satan did for thousands of years.

That's why, when Jesus came, He began to expose the actions of the devil; so that people would no longer fall into his subtle trap.

Jesus brought light to the enemy because for so long, he hid in the shadows. The devil needed to come out from the shadows and be revealed for what he truly is: stealer, killer, liar, deceiver and a destroyer. It was time that we were delivered as humanity from the evil one by exposing the truth.

Moreover, it was also time that we were delivered from our false idea of God. From a fallen viewpoint of Him, to the truth. God is good, holy, righteous, and He loves His children beyond measure. When we don't see God in this way, the truth of who He really is becomes fictional and untrue.

Happy is the one who seizes your infants and dashes them against rocks. Psalms 137:9 (NIV). That is not who our God is. He doesn't delight in the death of children. He warns that if any man harms children, *it would be better for them to be thrown into the sea with a millstone tied around their neck than to cause one of these little ones to stumble. Luke 17:2 (NIV).*

God is love. Jesus came to reveal who He is. When we factor in Jesus and God's nature throughout the New Testament, we begin to see that there's a bright light in the Old Testament.

We've been deceived over the years and veiled by falsehood. But now, the manifestation of the truth is being revealed and understood at a new level.

However, to read and understand the Bible in light of this truth, you have to give your life to Jesus and acknowledge that He is the exact representation of God the Father. Although this truth offends many religious people because they find it difficult to let go of their demonic view of God in the Old Testament.

Friend, God is love, and nothing has ever changed or will change who He is. **Everyone who loves has been born of God and knows God. Whoever does not love does not know God because God is love. 1 John 4:7-8 (NIV).** Therefore, we need to embrace this truth and live in the reality of the finished work of Christ.

First, I would like to say that I'm still not comfortable with raising the dead. I hate seeing death. Unfortunately, I can still feel intimidated by it at times. No doubt, I'm a work in progress. But the more I seek Him, the more I can see that it's His love that opens up the realm to see and understand the truth about immortality. Once you really see the truth - death is not there, it's gone! You simply don't give it any power anymore.

God's ultimate plan is for us to live. **John 3:16 (CEV), God loved the people of this world so much that he gave his only Son so that everyone who has faith in him will have eternal life and never really die.** It's abundant life. So, when someone does fall asleep, we can pray, and they can wake up.

When people choose to contend for life and not to embrace death (when they have just lost a loved one) the question people often ask us is, "What are we to do if we sense that the dead person doesn't want to come back to life, while we are praying to raise them?" The Word tells us, **Heal**

the sick, raise the dead, cleanse those who have leprosy, drive out demons. Freely you have received; freely give. Matthew 10:8 (NIV).

I love that question because it's an honest question, and I believe it's telling of our culture. It reveals our mindset that we prefer to go to heaven rather than bring heaven to earth. But Jesus didn't teach that way, neither did He think that way.

Death is never a friend that we are to make an agreement with under any circumstance.

In John 17, He taught that when He sent the disciples out that they would not leave the earth, but they'd be protected from the evil one. ***My prayer is not that you take them out of the world but protect them from the evil one. John 17:15 (NIV).***

So, He had a mindset of His disciples being victorious on earth, rather than going to heaven or desiring to go to heaven. Even the Apostle Paul confessed that it would be better for him to stay here on earth and finish his assigned work. ***I am torn between the two: I desire to depart and be with Christ, which is better by far; but it is necessary for you that I remain in the body. Convinced of this, I know that I will remain, and I will continue with all of you for your progress and joy in the faith. Philippians 1:23-25 (NIV).***

So, while we long for heaven, our real destiny is to bring heaven to earth. ***Your Kingdom come, your will be done, on earth as it is in heaven. Matthew 6:10 (NIV).***

We know our future, inevitably at some point, will be fully heaven. But death doesn't ever have to be a part of us, since it's not a part of who God is.

So, when people ask me, "What if they don't want to come back"? That question reflects so many things. It's a reflection that we need to be more Biblically minded. Otherwise, we empower into a culture that thinks about things like *man's will* and *wanting to die and go to heaven*, etc. On the contrary, a Biblical culture thinks about what the King wants, right? What does God want?

So, back to that scenario - if the person doesn't want to come back. They're thinking about what the dead want, rather than what the risen King wants. While it's understandable why they're asking, it also goes back to our fundamental issue of having a rapture-based theology rather than a victory-based theology.

Most people would want to escape and be done. Rather than establish God's Kingdom on earth as it is in heaven. It's a lot easier, but it's not our mandate. Someone has to stop that madness. We cannot let death keep winning. If we can begin to train people to think the Biblical way, the implication is when such people stand on the precipice of life and death, they won't be swayed by the circumstance of the situation. They will know their destiny and that their place is here on earth. They will not be agreeing with the spirit of death.

By the way, I just want to mention that several years ago, I was ministering to someone and the spirit of death had a grip on her. I audibly heard its voice saying, "I'll be back." No doubt, I know it's real. But I also know that we have the victory over it.

Let's go back and use the example when someone dies and they end up in heaven. They are now standing before the King. What if, He still has a plan for them on earth? What if, they were to tell Him that they want to partner with Him, for what He has for them; rather, than just wanting their own thing? If we teach people now, in this life, then fewer people will choose death. Does that make sense?

As for those people that are on this side, praying for a resurrection, we don't have to be concerned about what the dead want; we need to be concerned about what Jesus told us to do, which is in **Matthew 10:8 (NIV) Heal the sick, raise the dead, cleanse those who have leprosy, drive out demons. Freely you have received, freely give.** He told us to raise the dead. Right? So, I like that question because I think it's referring to our overall mindset. Our mindset predominantly in church culture is to hold on, until we can get out of this place. Jesus didn't think or teach that way. Death was never actually part of the equation, and it will never be. We cannot choose to be friends with death, ever! Do you see?

Just as man are destined to die once, and after that to face judgment. So, Christ was sacrificed once to take away the sins of many people; and he will appear a second time. Hebrews 9:27-29 (NIV).

People love to quote this Scripture. It often gives them an easy way out, to believe that death is part of God's plan for man. After all, praying for someone who is pronounced dead or on their deathbed is very awkward and uncomfortable; that is until their eyes are opened to more revelation of the truth. Then they get to see death as an enemy that's already been defeated—and they see how God is love and that there is no death in Him. It changes everything.

Let's look at that verse again.

- Just as people are destined to die once, (then there is a 'comma').

- The emphasis typically is put on verse 27, but the biblical emphasis is on, "So Christ was sacrificed." (verse 28). He was sacrificed once, to take away the sins of many.

- So, what this verse says is, before Christ, we were to die once and after that, face judgment.

And all that dwell upon the earth shall worship him, whose names are not written in the book of life of the Lamb slain from the foundation of the world. Revelation 13:8 (KJV).

So, even before Adam and Eve sinned in the Garden of Eden, God came up with the solution of sending Christ to clean up their mess. He was sacrificed once because we were supposed to die once. Our fate was to die once and after that to face judgment. So, Christ was sacrificed. He took our place; He took death away. Hallelujah!!!

Therefore, Hebrews 9:27-28 is talking about the reality that Christ has already died for you. The one death that we were supposed to experience, Jesus experienced it for us. He took away all sin. Now, if it said "that people should die twice", this would be fine. But we've already died with Christ; we do not need to die again. Christ was already sacrificed, and the fate that rested upon us to die rested upon Him, and now we're free. That is true love. God is Love. It would make no sense for Him to be part of death. Do you see?

So, if we just read verse 27, without factoring in verse 28, then the verse becomes a promise and a certainty. It's a declaration that death is unavoidable. But verse 28, makes it clear that the Bible isn't emphasizing the inevitability of death. It's emphasizing the cross and what Christ has done. Isn't that amazing?

Besides, the people that have the mindset of verse 27, also like to reference some of the following scriptures:

• *A time to be born, and a time to die. Ecclesiastes 3:2 (NIV)*

• *And the very hairs of your head are all numbered Matthew 10:30 (NIV).*

• *Then the Lord said, "My Spirit shall not abide in man forever, for he is flesh: his days shall be a hundred and twenty years." Genesis 6:3 (ESV).*

In Ecclesiastes, Jesus fulfilled the time to die. Now we get to live. Isn't that awesome?

Our days are numbered. Or, some say, that God numbers our days. That verse is not saying that God has a stopwatch on your life, where He's allotted you a certain amount of time on the earth. And when that time runs out, you're done! So, hurry up and do what you need to do quickly, before this clock runs out, or you're in trouble. No! That wouldn't make Him a loving God. Would you do that to your children? Would you kill them? Or, would you make them suffer and die? Would you afflict them? Or, would you give some a short life and give others a longer life? No sane person would do such a thing.

When the Bible talks about God numbering the days of our lives, it's not referring to Him waiting for each day to pass by until it gets to your last hour on earth. That's not what this is referring to. Because the Bible also talks about, "How God numbers each hair strand on our head." And that's not a foretelling of baldness. That's not what God is saying. What numbering the hairs on our head means is that He knows us intimately.

When it talks about numbering our days, it's not talking about the limited amount we have, and then He's anticipating to running out. It implies that He's well acquainted with every day of our life. **You have searched me, Lord, and you know me. You know when I sit and when I rise; you perceive my thoughts from afar. You discern my going out and my lying down; you are familiar with all my ways. Psalm 139:1-3 (NIV).** He's well acquainted with all of us. Isn't that beautiful?

How precious are your thoughts about me? O, God. They cannot be numbered! Were I to count them, they would outnumber the grains of the sand—when I awake, I am still with you. Psalm 139:17-18 (NIV).

He has billions and billions of beautiful thoughts towards us. None of them are about death. Can you believe that? Can you see that truth? He's so knowledgeable about every detail of our lives. Even how many hair strands we have on our head. Now that's a statement of intimacy. It's a statement of knowing you. Just as God numbering the days of your life, it's talking about Him being acquainted with every day that we're alive.

Genesis 6:3 (NASB), Then the Lord said, "My Spirit will not strive with man forever because he also is flesh; nevertheless, his days shall be one hundred and twenty years."

That's not God limiting the life of man to 120 years. Because even after that time, man lived longer than 120 years.

God is LOVE - He never actually created us to die

Note that these were all before the resurrection; how much more now?

Otherwise, Christ died for nothing.

So, the way we've traditionally read that verse has been skewed. It doesn't make any sense. Right?

If you read on after those verses, it begins to talk about the flood hitting the earth. So, what's happening is that the Holy Spirit is pleading with humanity and trying to convict people of sin. That's Him striving with man. He says, "I cannot strive with man forever." He's trying to warn man against sin, but people have hardened hearts, and they are resisting the conviction of the Spirit of God. Because the Spirit of God didn't just show up in Acts...He was also present throughout the Old Testament.

The Spirit of God was encouraging man to live righteously, but they didn't listen. The result is that in one hundred and twenty years, the flood would hit. One hundred and twenty years after that, we see that the flood swept and covered the entire earth. So, it's a warning and a prophecy of the flood, and it's not a limit on the life span of man. Jesus came to give life in abundance and to defeat death.

It's really about maturing as a believer.

We must believe.

Do you believe?

Seeing for the first time is so exciting.

FOUR

The Truth Sets Us Free

In this chapter, fasten your seatbelts because we are going on a fun ride. You will get jolted with new truths. At other times, you will be shocked. But throughout all of it, your spirit will have the best time. Like a roller coaster ride, throw your doubts in the air and feel the freshness of the Holy Spirit.

As you read further, you'll feel the frequency of His love permeate throughout your entire body. Also, get ready for a feast (as you eat from His Word). The good news is that you can come back as often as you want. You can also ask the Holy Spirit to reveal new dimensions of truth each time you flip back the pages of this book and read His Word.

Watchman Nee once said, *"To secure one's freedom, the Christian must experience God's light, which is God's truth."* I believe there is no greater quest than understanding the truth concealed in God's Word about us.

King David once prayed, **Open my eyes [to spiritual truth] so that I may behold wonderful things from your law. Psalm 119:18 (AMP).** Indeed, some of you reading this may or may not yet be comfortable with what the Word says about immortality. I pray that as you continue with me on this adventure, in search of the truth, the Lord will shed new light into your heart, which will culminate in a life-changing experience for you.

Original by
Rita Hinton

Are you ready to experience His truth at a new level? Are you prepared today to receive a divine inoculation of the Word that will launch you into a higher dimension of joy, peace, and hope? If you're ready…let's dive in with the understanding that this adventure is solely an experience between you and Him.

But the natural [unbelieving] man does not accept the things [the teachings and revelations] of the Spirit of God, for they are foolishness [absurd and illogical] to him; and he is incapable of understanding them because they are spiritually discerned and appreciated, [and

he is unqualified to judge spiritual matters]. 1 Corinthians 2:14 (AMP).

Therefore, as you expose yourself to the great light from the frequency of His Word, you may start to feel your mind reciting the lyrics of uncertainties like Mary, **How can this be...? Luke 1:34 (NKJV).** But here is my recommendation to you. As God begins to unveil His truth to you, do not shut down any of the revelation, simply because you can't figure it all out, just yet. But instead, let your spirit be in agreement with God's Word, and you will begin to sense His unexplainable peace.

> Jesus looked at them and said,
> "With man this is impossible,
> but **WITH GOD ALL THINGS ARE POSSIBLE.**"
>
> **Matthew 19:26 (NIV)**

In this chapter, I want to go deeper than I normally do. I sense that I'm to release what God has put on my heart to encourage you and to bring you to a new realm of truth and freedom.

Let me share an encounter with you that I had several years ago. It was a period when I had developed an insatiable hunger for more of God's truth. The desire was somewhat frustrating because I couldn't pinpoint what the spiritual hunger was all about. Initially, it felt like a mystery, a sense of emptiness and dissatisfaction, in my spiritual life. I knew there was more, but I couldn't get to it.

One day, I came across some teachings from Kirby de Lanerolle, that started filling the void that I had inside. Soon, the Holy Spirit began to guide me into new depths of revelation for what I was longing for in my spirit, even though I was unable to articulate my experience with words at that time.

I immediately started going through a time of tremendous spiritual revamping, and the results have been nothing short of amazing.

During that season, I had to be careful not to shut the door of my heart. I had to choose to receive the revelation even though it was so-called, "out there." I also had to choose not to turn off the flow of insight just because I couldn't figure it all out.

I didn't bail-out just because those around me didn't see what I was seeing. I didn't seek people to cheer me on. I knew that most of them would be offended or simply not understand. I was confident in my spirit that this was God revealing remarkable truths to me, that would forever change the course of my life.

After this destiny-altering experience, new doors of opportunity started opening up. Which allowed me to travel on several international trips. where I met up with like-minded people. When I traveled to the Wow Church in Sri Lanka, it was so encouraging to share my revelation with people that were not limiting God in their lives.

Kirby, Fiona, and Mel welcomed me with the love of Jesus. Their culture in Sri Lanka is amazing. Kirby and Fiona's leadership surpasses anything I have ever seen and experienced in my life. The anointing that is on their lives has forever changed my own life. They are open to new dimensions of the Holy Spirit, like I have never seen before and yet, I have read about it in His Word.

For with God, nothing will be impossible. Luke 1:37 (NKJV). When I visited, they were having people starting to train for marathons at well over the age of sixty. Simultaneously, some others were pushing the boundaries by opening up their new businesses after sixty-five and as early as eighteen years of age. Others, were also led by the Holy Spirit to fast for long periods of time and to live off Communion, while training vigorously for different marathons and various other sporting events.

You may ask, how is this possible at a time when currently, several diseases and viruses are popping up unannounced and streaming down thousands of lives all over the world? How were they able to pull such an unprecedented feat, some without any food? Well, the answers are all found in the Holy Spirit (His Word) and having a relationship with Him. Knowing the truth is what sets us all free. **Then you will know the truth, and the truth will set you free. John 8:32 (NIV).**

I'm so thankful for my new extended family in Sri Lanka, who continue to express God's love and truth to the world. They believe in long life (as promised by God in His Word). It's awesome to witness the Scriptures coming alive at a whole new level. Could God be that good? Could His Word be true to a level of being above and beyond amazing?

I remember a while back someone was joking around and asking the question, "What would your Bible look like if you were to cut out all the Scriptures that you didn't feel comfortable with regarding immortality?

Would it look like Swiss Cheese?

By profession, I'm neither a Scientist nor a Doctor, and I am not a Theologian. But the revelation that I've received from God has given me answers that sometimes I will see in Headline News. It varies with new findings regarding the human body, life, nutrition, immortality, etc. Only God knows the end from the beginning. He reveals amazing revelation to His children when we seek Him. **The secret things belong to the LORD our God, but the things revealed belong to us and to our children forever, that we may follow all the words of this law. Deuteronomy 29:29 (NIV).**

Several years ago, I was attending an exposition about "Technology Evolution." They had an old manual typewriter. They also had the evolution of the electric one, and so on.

God immediately put on my heart that when people first invented the typewriter, they were so happy. It was exciting for them. Even though they had to use a piece of carbon paper to make a copy. And they really couldn't afford to make a typo, otherwise, it was a big procedure to correct a mistake. Nevertheless, God was rejoicing with them, too, even though He knew that one day there would be computers, smartphones and countless advanced smart gadgets. The point is that there is so much more than we can ever imagine. He knows the end from the beginning. So, when He tells us that He has defeated death. We need to believe Him.

Recently this was in the headline news.

If science is coming up with these types of discoveries; how much more has God already done for us?

Anytime we hear of things that we can't quite figure out; we try to dismiss them because it's not comfortable. Our reactions are probably very similar, or the same, as those who were using typewriters back in the 1960s. If they would have read a newspaper article that would have explained the features of a smartphone. Basically, how you will hold it in your hand and speak to it, and it will respond and give you answers instantaneously. They would not have believed it and they would have dismissed it. No doubt, it would have sounded as foreign as immortality might sound to many of us. Yet, it's the truth. Who wants to have a God that they can figure everything out about Him? Yet, when we don't have it all figured out...we don't usually believe. There is so much more, than just living by our five senses.

In the same vein, God always has so much more. We just need to believe and stop trying to figure it all out on our own with our limited mindset... it's called faith. The point is we will always have faith in something. We usually will have faith in God, or we will have faith in Satan. It's always one or the other.

ABUNDANT LIFE IN CHRIST

God's plan and purpose for all of us, is not for us to be saved, then die, and then go to heaven. No! On the contrary, His desire is for us to manifest the realities of heaven here on earth. Above all else, He wants us to experience abundant life here on earth, right now!

But we need to change our way of thinking to His truths.

Here are some questions with quick drive-thru answers. They are to be used as seeds. Then you can let the Word water them and watch them grow in your life.

Seed Question #1 Why do we believe more in death than immortality?

Answer: It's the world's pattern, and it's easier and more comfortable to just believe in death, even though we have to dismiss what the Word tells us.

Jesus said in **John 10:10 (NKJV), "The thief does not come except to steal, and to kill and to destroy. I have come that they may have life and that they may have it more abundantly."**

Seed Question #2 Why do we believe more in lack than in abundance?

Answer: It's easier to just believe in what we see. It's more comfortable and that's what most people believe, too.

Seed Question #3 Why do we believe in sickness more than healing?

Answer: As soon as we get a symptom, we turn to fear (death mentality). We then research it hoping it's not bad. We never do research because we think it's good. So, we always automatically believe in sickness. Faith is challenging when the symptoms are not looking positive. So, once again, it's easier to just believe in what we see. It's more comfortable and more convenient.

The mind governed by the flesh is death, but the mind governed by the Spirit is life and peace. Romans 8:6 (NIV).

Seed Question # 4 Why do we believe Satan more than God?

Answer: This question touches the depths of our being. Can you feel it? Yes! We have been living on a foundational belief system of death, which manifests as fear, worry, etc. Dying is easier than standing for "life" especially when you reach a certain age. It is what we have been programmed to think and believe; regardless what His Word says. This too, is easier and more comfortable.

For those who live according to the flesh set their minds on things of the flesh, but those who live according to the Spirit set their minds on the things of the Spirit. Romans 8:5 (ESV).

Did you notice that "comfort" was part of all the answers? **For the flesh desires what is contrary to the Spirit, and the Spirit what is contrary to the flesh. They are in conflict with each other, so that you are not to do whatever you want. Galatians 5:17 (NIV).**

Everything that does not come from faith is sin. Romans 14:23b (ESV). And sin is the root of death.

But now the door has been opened. We are starting to see the light, as the picture below symbolizes. Therefore, a crown is being placed on our heads, representing our true identity. We are awakening to the truth. It's always been there; it's just that we are now finally in agreement with His Word.

We are children of the Almighty. He loves us unconditionally. We are not prodigal children. Death is not our inheritance, and it never will be. We get to choose *to believe or not to believe,* His Word.

Jesus said to her "I am the resurrection and the life. The one who believes in me will live even though they die. And whoever lives by believing in me will never die. Do you believe this?" John 11:25-26 (NIV).

Let's now go into the book of John Chapter 4, where a discussion ensued between Jesus, His disciples, and the Samaritan woman. They had a stop at Jacob's well in Samaria, and Jesus sent His disciples to get food. Jesus was about to demonstrate and teach a dimension of truth that has somewhat been bypassed by most all of us...until now.

So, the disciples left to get food, and when they returned, Jesus' response was beyond what they were expecting. He said to them, **"I have food to eat that you know nothing about." Then his disciples said to each other, "Could someone have brought him food?" John 4:32-33 (NIV).**

Let's look at it again. **I have food to eat that you know nothing about. John 4:32 (NIV).** Is this another piece of revelation encompassed with immortality?

The truth is, once we continue to go deeper into the revelation of immortality and start living that truth, I guarantee that we will not have the same mindset about food, age, bucket lists, and sickness that we have today. Our minds will be transformed into His truth. Not having a death mentality, changes everything. Once you start getting glimpses of what that looks like - you will really see, how we've all lived in such bondage, to Satan's lies.

Understanding that we are now starting to see into this truth, is so encouraging. No doubt there is so much more forthcoming. But we can't reject what God is showing us today. ***It is the glory of God to conceal a thing: but the honor of kings is to search out a matter. Proverbs 25:2 (KJV).*** We are redeemed as kings and priests, so we have a responsibility to search out the deep things of God, so that we can manifest our redemptive provisions on the earth.

Jesus said in ***Matthew 7:7 (NIV). "Ask, and it will be given to you; seek, and you will find; knock, and the door will be opened to you."*** The subject of 'immortality' may still feel like it is foreign and yet He tells us, ***Now to him who is able to do far more abundantly than all that we ask or think, according to the power at work within us, Ephesians 3:20 (ESV).***

But when He, the Spirit of truth, comes, he will guide you into all the truth. He will not speak on his own; he will speak only what he hears, and he will tell you what is yet to come. John 16:13 (NIV). So, when you start seeking and searching Scriptures about 'immortality' with the help of the Holy Spirit, your eyes will begin to open to different revelations and truths from His Word that you never saw before, even though you may have read it a hundred times in the past.

You will start to understand His love more than ever. It changes and affects everything in your life, to include peace, love, joy, healing, abundance, revelation, etc. Your relationship with Him will keep getting stronger.

His Word has so many levels of revelation. ***Matthew 4:1-4 (NIV),*** the Scripture says, ***Then Jesus was led by the Spirit into the wilderness to be tempted by the devil. After fasting forty days and forty nights, he was hungry. The tempter came to him and said, "If you are the Son of God, tell these stones to become bread." Jesus answered, "It is written: 'Man shall not live on bread alone, but on every Word that comes from the mouth of God."***

Jesus told the enemy that there is authority and power in God's Word. ***In the beginning was the Word, and the Word was with God, and*** *the Word was God. He was with God in the beginning. Through him all things were made; without him nothing was made that has been made. In him was life, and that life was the light of men. John 1:1-4 (NIV).*

> **ALL**
> that exists today came to be...
>
> by the **WORD** of **GOD**
>
> **Ref: John 1:14 (NIV).**

His Word is a vibrational frequency that we can't see with our physical eyes. It is not visible, yet it is present, alive, and powerful.

Another piece of the mystery for immortality is to speak His Word (life) as we abide in Him (Love).

Now there was a Pharisee, a man named Nicodemus, a member of the Jewish ruling council. He came to Jesus at night and said, "Rabbi, we know that you are a teacher who has come from God. For no one could perform the signs you are doing of God were not with him." Jesus replied, "Very truly, I tell you, no one can see the kingdom of God unless they are born again." "How can someone be born when they are old?" Nicodemus asked. "Surely they cannot enter a second time into their mother's womb to be born!" Jesus answered, "Very truly I tell you, no one can enter the kingdom of God unless they are born of water and the Spirit. Flesh gives birth to flesh, but the Spirit gives birth to Spirit. You should not be surprised at my saying, 'you must be born again.' The wind blows wherever it pleases. You hear its sound, but you cannot tell where it comes from or where it is going. So it is with everyone born of the Spirit". John 3:1-8 (NIV).

He says, "Don't you know that you can only hear the sound of it? It is not visible. It is not something tangible like food, clothing, or money. It is a subtle energy that comes to you, and once it is planted in you, the cycle of salvation is complete, and you become born again. That means you will not be of natural origin anymore; you will be of an exceptional kind. However, this experience comes through vibrational form, just like what you are experiencing as you read His Word in this book.

Can you remember how you got saved? For most people, it was when someone spoke the Word. You could only hear the sound and not see it (not visible), but something changed in you. **Therefore, if anyone is in Christ, the new creation has come. The old has gone, the new is here. 2 Corinthians 5:17 (NIV).**

When we expose ourselves to the vibrations from the Word through the Spirit, our body is quickened. **The Spirit gives life; the flesh counts for nothing. The words I have spoken to you—they are full of the Spirit and life. John 6:63 (NIV).**

In the beginning, there was a 'sound and a frequency' with the Word during creation. Jesus is this Word. There is a sound of the Spirit that when it comes to you, it regenerates you. Not just in your spirit but throughout your entire body. Therefore, we must always continue to choose to abide in that frequency of love. God is love.

Needless to say, that in our everyday lives, we will continue to meet negative frequencies (death) that people carry, but we can't allow their views (words of death) to rub off on us. We must choose not to submit to their counsel. Jesus came to give life, and His Word is truth. **Jesus answered, "I am the way and the truth and the life" John 14:6 (NIV).**

We must also be wise about the company we keep. There is a warning sign in **Hebrews 3:12-14 (KJV). *Take heed, brethren, lest there be in any of you an evil heart of unbelief, in departing from the living God. But exhort one another daily, while it is called today, lest any of you be hardened through the deceitfulness of sin, for we are made partakers of Christ if we hold the beginning of our confidence steadfast unto the end.***

> # EXHORT
> # One Another
> # DAILY
>
> ### Hebrew 3:13 (NIV)

Today, the world is already condemned, and people carry different frequencies - which many are rooted in death (in their souls). If we don't stay in the anointing (love frequency), we may be impacted by their storms.

On the other hand, if we hang around with people who believe in immortality and they heal the sick and do miracles, we will probably want to heal the sick and do miracles too. That is the frequency, sound, and vibrational frequency of the dominion of the King. You can be a victim, or you can be a victor. We always get to choose life or death. That choice is still ours to make daily. It's either one or the other.

For our struggle is not against flesh and blood, but against the rulers, against the authorities, against the powers of this dark world, and against the spiritual forces of evil in the heavenly realms. Ephesians 6:12 (NIV).

The heavenly realms are within us. So, it's not a foreign place that is far, far away…it's all inside of us. Therefore, it's imperative to understand that the Kingdom is within us.

Behold, the Kingdom of God is within you. Luke 17:21b (KJV).

You must know your position and your true identity. You are born again and God has given you His incorruptible seed. You are immortal. **For you have been born again, not of perishable seed, but of imperishable, through the living and enduring word of God. 1 Peter 1:23 (NIV).** The seed that He has given you is a seed from heaven. This seed is incorruptible and undefiled; it's a mono gene in your spirit, and it keeps growing unless you subject it to earthly afflictions (mindsets).

Today, doctors are finding out more about electroceuticals and the bioelectrical value that you have, and how it can be transferred. For instance, when you lay your hands on the sick, subtle energy is released. We have called it the power of the Holy Spirit. If a small electric current can change and rewire the brain, imagine how powerful our electromagnetic wave is. That is why Jesus said; **"but whoever drinks the water I give them will never thirst. Indeed, the water I give them will become in** *them a spring of water welling up to eternal life." John 4:14 (NIV).*

Let us go back to John 4, and look at it through the eyes of frequency and energy.

But He said to them, "I have food to eat that you know nothing about." Then his disciples said to each other, "Could someone have brought him food?" "My food," said Jesus, "is to do the will of him who sent me and to finish his work. John 4:32-34 (NIV).

What do you see?

What's interesting is that Jesus never spent any time or energy trying to meet the FDA's daily requirements for any of His food intake. Nor, did He impose it on anyone else. One of His disciples was a doctor. That topic of needing certain foods with daily requirements was never an issue or a necessity...isn't that interesting? But He does say, that there is a food that we do not know of. I believe part of it is feeding off Communion. **Whoever eats my flesh and drinks my blood has eternal life, and I will raise them up at the last day. John 6:54 (NIV).**

What I'm learning about food and fasting, is that we just can't fast and not replace it with spiritual food. Otherwise, we starve, and that's when it's not healthy. That's simply the act of starving without physical or spiritual nourishment. Nothing that we do should be based on our own performance. We are now under grace. So, we need to start seeking what it means to live off spiritual food.

> **FASTING**
>
> is letting go of physical food &
> replacing it with **SPIRITUAL FOOD**
>
> -SL

How then shall they call on Him in whom they have not believed? And how shall they believe in Him of whom they have not heard? And how shall they hear without a preacher? Romans 10:14 (NIV).

Once we receive revelation, we need to release the sound by speaking it. We need to preach it. We need to talk about it to people. Too often, people fail because they have revelation (truth) inside of them, but they are not releasing it. However, when this frequency is released to others, they also receive the same impartation, and it becomes stronger.

God gives life, and He has defeated death. If death is defeated, we need to believe Him.

I'll be transparent by saying that immortality still sounds foreign to me, as far as living it out daily. It's also confusing at times, and it feels so far-fetched. Yet, I see it over and over again in His Word. My spirit is super excited and full of joy. I now find myself sometimes imagining what it would be like see people completely free from death. You might think that's strange, right? Yet, people imagine certain people dying, and no one thinks that's strange.

How do you think Jesus feels when we agree with death?

We know without a shadow of a doubt, that God does not want death, for any of us. He is love. He is not a murderer, and there is no death in Him.

I no longer want Satan to keep stealing, killing, and destroying. I don't want to keep seeing people (including children) dying when I know that it is not His will. Death is never from a loving father, and anyone who inflicts death is called a murderer. Our God is not a murderer.

So why not seek, receive, and believe this truth that He has defeated death? Why should we continue to be a victim of what He has already defeated, just because it doesn't sound conventional? Why dismiss His truth because we can't figure it all out?

Here is my interpretation of a story from Kirby…

One day the Lord put on his mind to look at a water pipe in the kitchen. The water pipe had a small leak which created water to drip on the floor. Then He took him to another scene and showed him a picture in his mind of someone mopping the floor repeatedly. Then He said, "That is what you are doing when you are praying for the sick. You are just mopping the floor, but the pipe is still leaking. It will just keep needing more mopping."

The root cause of why people are sick and die has not changed. We all need to turn from our old ways and seek God and invest in His Word. He will always guide us *step by step*. We cannot live by the standards of the world and expect to walk in immortality. No! You have to draw the line and turn to the Word, the truth. **For to set the mind on the flesh is death, but to set the mind on the Spirit is life and peace. Romans 8:6 (ESV).**

Now, get ready for your brain to tilt and for your spirit to rejoice; this will be fun. You will feel your flesh say, "No way." But your Spirit will rejoice.

Let me share some 'brain tilts' that have impacted my life.

The natural person does not accept the things of the **Spirit of God**, for they are folly to Him, and He is not able to understand them because they are **spiritually discerned**.

1 Corinthians 2:14 (ESV)

Brain Tilt #1

It is worth mentioning again that some of my friends overseas don't need to eat for very long periods of time to stay healthy, alive, and active. Through amazing revelation, they simply feed on the Holy Communion. *And he took bread, gave thanks and broke it, and gave it to them, saying, "This is my body given for you, do this in remembrance of me." In the same way, after the supper he took the cup, saying "this cup is the new covenant in my blood, which is poured out for you. Luke 22: 19-20 (NIV).*

Brain Tilt #2

Another preacher in Africa, hasn't had anyone in his congregation die in the past ten years. He believes that the *spirit of death* has been demolished. He stands in the faith that no one will die under his watch. So, he gives Satan no power. Death has been defeated. It's in the Word, so why cut it out? Why not believe the truth? Why not stand for the truth? Why ignore the truth, simply because it's not comfortable?

But it has now been revealed through the appearing of our Savior, Christ Jesus, who has destroyed death and has brought life and immortality to light through the gospel. 2 Timothy 1:10 (NIV).

Brain Tilt #3

I have a friend named Sandesh, who believes in praying over his food. He is also thankful for the lives that were laid down for his meal. Then, when he partakes in eating, he does so, with a consciousness of his body receiving the right nutrients from the meal. With a clear conscience he believes and knows that he is one with God and that nothing from the outside can defile him. The biggest revelation is unlike most people because he can eat anything and he doesn't gain weight. He doesn't need to exercise to maintain his weight. I believe this is another key, to so much more.

Only believe. Why? **According to your faith let it be done to you. Matthew 9:29b (NIV).**

Brain Tilt #4

Someone else, I know named Chris, will usually go for certain periods of time just feeding off Communion. When he does, he believes that *holy Communion* has all the nutrients that his body needs. That is precisely the results he gets. He doesn't feel hungry, and he does not lose weight, yet he feels healthy.

Brain Tilt #5

Some of the mystics that lived a long time ago would tap into so much heavenly glory on earth. When they died their bodies never deteriorated. There is documented proof. You can research it.

Enoch walked faithfully with God; then he was no more, because God took him away. Genesis 5:24 (NIV). So, his body never died.

Brain Tilt #6

Tyler G. Johnson has researched many Saints from the past. He tells of the story of when a group had gathered, and they had finished eating fish. One had the skeleton part of the fish still on his plate. They believed in the power of God and spoke His Word to bring back the fish. And that's exactly what happened. I love that story because I really do believe in the power of the Word. We can bless or curse.

For in him all things were created: things in heaven and on earth, visible and invisible, whether thrones or powers or rulers or authorities; all things have been created through him and for him. Colossian 1:16 (NIV). His Word created everything. We are one with Him.

Scientists recently published an article that had the headline – ***Matter will be created from light within a year,*** claim Scientists. If Scientists can do this, how much more can we, with the Word of God? God's Word is the highest frequency.

And I will do whatever you ask in my name, so that the Father may be glorified in the Son. You may ask me for anything in my name, and I will do it. John 14:13-14 (NIV).

Do you believe?

Although, I haven't personally received the revelation yet for some of what I have just mentioned in the "brain tilts", especially feeding only on the Holy Communion, I am asking God to keep showing me His truth.

Recently, I started to see and understand in my spirit that food is really for pleasure. The science part of what we've been programmed to believe is not what Jesus modeled for us. The mystery of Communion is a huge deal.

The Scriptures talk about food that we do not know of, and the good news is that our spiritual eyes are opening up. It is the beginning of something remarkable, and you are a part of it, too! The good news is that you are destined for a time such as this…the best of times. You are so blessed.

If you declare with your mouth, "Jesus is Lord," and believe in your heart that God raised him from the dead, you will be saved. Romans 10:9 (NIV).

The definition for saved in the Strong's is 'Sozo' which means delivered out of danger and into safety. God rescuing believers from the penalty and power of sin and into His provisions (safety).

When we believe, we tap into the frequency of protection from the power of sin and death.

Overhearing what they said, Jesus told him, "Don't be afraid; just believe." Mark 5:36 (NIV).

I say to you also, JUST BELIEVE!

"If we find ourselves with a desire that nothing in this world can satisfy, the most probable explanation is that we were made for another world."
– C.S. Lewis

Your kingdom come, you will be done, on earth as it is in heaven. Matthew 6:10 (ESV).

Do you believe?

Pastor Sung Han

FIVE

Science Confirms The Word

The World's Quest for Immortality
Authored by Pastor Sung Han

"Immortality, Inc. - Chip Walter on Big Tech's Immortality Quest

How Silicon Valley titans came to believe aging was a disease that could be cured"[1]

"Scientists Claim We Might be Immortal in 17 Years - This is How"[2]

Scientists Could One Day Make Humans Immortal"[3]

Yes, you read those headlines correctly. These are a few of many legitimate articles currently circulating throughout various media outlets around the world. What's intriguing is that the headlines are not just catchy attention-garnering phrases, but the substance of the articles themselves reflect the brainiacs and industry titans of the world's belief that immortality is within man's reach, albeit through science and technology.

As technology advances, the scientific theory of immortality becomes less sci-fi and distant, with many believing that it will become attainable in as little as two decades. With that in mind, they have already invested billions of dollars towards the quest for eternal life. It seems the advancements of science always point to what the Word of God has been trying to reveal all along.

One of the more well-known companies in the "immortality" industry is called Calico (California Life Company). They are currently conducting research and development into what they phrase as "solving death" through anti-aging. Google's founders Sergey Brin and Larry Page pioneered this company by bringing on Arthur Levinson, the chairman of Apple, to oversee this business. They've raised up to 1.5 billion dollars from seasoned investors to launch this endeavor.

The company employs some of the brightest minds in the world, such as J. Graham Ruby, Ph.D., who holds a doctorate from MIT. He's just one of many highly decorated researchers on the Calico team. Calico has been very secretive about their research, but they did release a study in January of 2018 titled, "Naked mole-rat mortality rates defy Gompertzian laws by not increasing with age"[1]. Essentially, they announced that the naked mole-rat is a "non-aging mammal" and could help unlock the door to eternal life or, at the very least extreme longevity of life.

> **Hoping to solve DEATH Thru Anti-aging?**
>
> **There is GOOD NEWS...**
>
> **God has already given us the answers**

Ironically, as Jesus proclaimed that the Kingdom of Heaven is near, Sierra Sciences is now proclaiming that the cure for aging is near. Sierra's own mission statement states, "Develop a drug that will induce the production of Telomerase to lengthen human Telomeres and therefore reverse our aging process, as well as cure diseases linked to aging."

Our cells are innately designed to reproduce after themselves perpetually; however, as cells reproduce, telomeres, which are protective caps on the end of DNA molecules, shorten, causing gradual decay or corruption of the cell, which in turn causes aging. Sierra is out to prevent this decay from occurring by keeping the telomeres intact. By doing so, Bill Andrews, Ph.D. at Sierra Sciences, boldly states, "Aging can be controlled and stopped, a statement solidly grounded in good science, which makes it both verifiable and demonstrable."

Elizabeth Parrish, CEO of BioViva, has already undergone regenerative therapy on herself, now that's someone who stands behind their product! Amazingly, she is already showing signs of restoring her telomere length by as much as thirty years. Founder of Rejuvenate Bio and also a Harvard professor has already doubled the life span of mice using gene therapy. Aubrey de Grey, an author, and biomedical gerontologist, is the Chief

Science Officer at SENS Research Foundation. He spoke during a TED Talk claiming that he has drawn a roadmap to defeat biological aging. *He provocatively proposes that the first human beings who will live to 1,000 years old have already been born"4*. He reported, "I think it's reasonable to suppose that one could oscillate between being biologically 20 and biologically 25 indefinitely."

> **NOW UNTO HIM THAT IS ABLE TO DO EXCEEDINGLY ABUNDANTLY ABOVE ALL THAT WE ASK OR THINK, ACCORDING TO THE POWER THAT WORKETH IN US**
> Ephesians 3:20 (KJV)

Currently, there are numerous organizations, including highly esteemed universities, that are investing extensive time and resources into discovering the cure for death. Whether it's genetic therapies as previously discussed, nanobot technology (where tiny robots will float along your bloodstream and make repairs to the body as necessary), virtual machines (where we can upload our consciousness into a cloud-like storage which can then be downloaded into android bodies), cryogenics, or cryonic and ozone saunas, the common underlying thread is the wide held belief that humans have the capacity to live forever. Deep in the heart of mankind, we have the innate God-given desire to become more like the image of God, and mankind yearns to operate as God originally designed from the beginning.

In **Genesis 1:26 (NIV)**, God said, *"Let Us make man in Our image, according to Our likeness; and let them rule over the fish of the sea* *and over the birds of the sky and over the cattle and over all the earth, and over every creeping thing that creeps on the earth."* You can see this immortal longing to be God-like all around us, especially in the imagination of humankind as often expressed in cinematics, comics, books, superheroes, and of course, the technological advances that the visionaries of this world are developing to propel humankind into the future.

Immortality – it's in the Word.

For God so loved the world that he gave his one and only Son, that whoever believes in him shall not perish[die] but have eternal [immortal] life. John 3:16 (NIV), emphasis added. This is probably one of the most widely known and recited verses in the Bible, as well as one of the most misunderstood. When I was first introduced to the "Christian" faith, I was told that Jesus Christ came to die for my sins so that I may be forgiven and when I died, I could then go to heaven (it should be noted that the "good news" in the new testament is hardly about going to heaven, it is about heaven coming to earth but we'll save that for a later part of this chapter). I would venture to say that every single person reading this has grown up with an embedded belief that death is inevitable, that it is just a normal part of the cycle of life. We see death all around us, whether our great grandparents, other family members, friends, associates, co-workers, or even our pets.

Death has been so engrained into all of human existence that most people universally accept it as reality. Consequently, approaching scripture with a mental gridlock that death is inevitable forces us to spiritualize verses like John 3:16, necessitating "eternal life" to be preceded by death, even though that idea is not in the text itself.

Could it be that the Bible is saying we don't need to die a physical death to go to heaven? The seeming reality of death permeates every aspect of our existence. Imagine for a moment that you grew up seeing very little death around you. You would go visit your great, great, great grandparents often to get spoiled with ice cream, toys, and no curfews. "Short term" financial planning would consist of 100-year terms. Nobody would joke about your age until you reached 800 years old (the isle for birthday cards and anniversaries would need to be expanded to an entire store!). Bucket lists would be termed "Life to-do lists," and "vintage" would take on a whole new meaning.

We must become cognizant of how entrenched our culture and lives are around a limited life expectancy and inevitable death. Insurance, retirement ages, senior benefits all point to it. Loss of energy, endurance, physical strength, and overall wellness are an accepted result of age. We joke about our bodies "falling apart" after 40 and continue to program our minds towards this end. However, if we are able to remove the paradigm of unavoidable death from our thinking, as many scientists have already done, it will change every aspect of our life, including the way we interpret scripture.

If we read the same John 3:16 verse in this new light, with immortality being a divinely attainable gift hard-wired in our design, it will most definitely mean something entirely different. We have colored scripture with a dimmed understanding of the potential of life in our beings, and God is revealing His truth by His Spirit. Imagine how our purpose and existence would alter if death wasn't able to rob us of time to accomplish the rich destinies He has created us for.

As believers, we can embrace the potential of our design and forego the expensive gene therapies to accomplish it. Just as many believers today believe in healing through prayer and not necessarily depending solely on modern medicine, my hope and prayer is that the body of Christ would begin to step into faith in the same way regarding everlasting life. In other words, believers that take John 3:16 and other scriptures promising "eternal life" at face value.

> Whoever **BELIEVES** in **HIM**
>
> Shall **NOT PERISH**
>
> But have **EVERLASTING** Life
>
> **John 3:16 (NIV)**

Instead of altering the meaning of the verse to match our cultural currents, the time is coming for believers to stand firm in the truly eternal word of God and not alter our own interpretation through the lens of un-renewed minds of unbelief. Amazingly, one of the most prevalent (and most overlooked) themes of the Bible is centered on immortal life right here on earth! I encourage you to take a moment, close your eyes, and ask the Holy Spirit to remove any preconceived notions of death and for fresh eyes to see and hearts to understand. Then hang on to your latte and read on because we are just getting started!

Bread from Heaven

In John 6:22-69, we see an interesting dialogue between a very large crowd of people and Jesus. The subject about food came up because of a miracle that Jesus did to feed the large crowd that was following him. After the crowd was fed, they sought after Jesus even more fervently. Jesus responds to them by saying, "***I tell you the truth, you want to be with me because I fed you, not because you understood the miraculous signs. But don't be so concerned about perishable things like food. Spend your energy seeking the eternal life that the Son of Man can***

give you. For God, the Father has given me the seal of his approval."
John 6:26-27 (NLV) *emphasis mine.* The crowd then demanded a sign as a prerequisite for them to believe in Jesus and stated that in the past, Moses, whom they already believed in, provided bread from heaven for the people to eat (referring to the Israelite's journey through the wilderness after they were freed from Egyptian slavery, around 1446 BC). Jesus' answer to this was that Moses didn't give the people the bread from heaven but that it was actually his Father. But that now, the Father is offering the true bread from heaven, meaning Jesus Christ himself. This bread gives eternal (immortal) life to the world, given to anyone who is willing to partake of it.

The crowd started murmuring because Jesus was stating that He himself was the bread that came down from heaven! Disagreements arose because some argued that they knew where Jesus came from and knew who his father and mother were, so how could he have come from heaven? At this point, Jesus gives a remarkable answer; **"I tell you the truth, anyone who believes has eternal life. Yes, I am the bread of life! Your ancestors ate manna in the wilderness, but they all died. Anyone who eats the bread from heaven, however, will never die. I am the living bread that came down from heaven. Anyone who eats this bread will live forever; and this bread, which I will offer so the world may live, is my flesh." John 6:47-51(NLT).**

> *I am the*
> **LIVING BREAD**
> *whoever eats this*
> *Bread*
> **WILL LIVE FOREVER**
>
> **John 6:51 (NIV)**

Don't worry, Jesus wasn't advocating cannibalism here! The flesh he was referring to was his divine or heavenly body for anyone who believes to come to union with – more on that shortly. The point of me sharing this passage is that Jesus gave an example of what he meant by eternal life. He said that their ancestors ate the manna (bread) in the wilderness, but they all died. Was this a spiritual death, or was this a physical death? This death he refers to was very physical indeed. In the same manner, the next words out of his mouth is that anyone who eats the true bread from heaven will never die. Just as the death of the ancestors was a very physical death, the "never die" is referring to a very physical immortality, not a "spiritual" immortality as we have been conditioned to believe.

The Immortal Gene (Seed)

Who has saved us and called us with a holy calling, not according to our works, but according to His own purpose and grace which was given to us in Christ Jesus before time began, but has now been revealed by the appearing of our Savior Jesus Christ, who has abolished death and brought life and immortality to light through the gospel. 2 Timothy 1:9-10 (NKJV) emphasis mine.

The gospel or good news is that Jesus Christ came to save us. Most of us have been taught that salvation saves us from going to Hell after death. But it is so, so much more than that! Salvation is to save us from perishing, aka dying! Save us from sickness and disease. Save us from mental and emotional anguish. Save us from any aspect of life that is not flourishing and prospering.

The interesting thing is that this grace was given to us in Christ before time began. In other words, human beings have had access to immortal life this whole time. Why aren't people living forever then? That's a fair question. There is at least one person in recorded biblical history who has not died, Enoch. However, besides very rare instances, humans, in general, have all perished, although the potential to live forever has been there all long.

However, consider this: humans have had access to harnessing solar energy since the dawn of time. Although the use of solar energy can date back to over a millennium (the uses were more primitive such as sunrooms for capturing warmth, reflective and intensified beams for battle and fires), it's only in the last 50 to 60 years that humankind has begun to capture the potential of the sun's energy for large scale energy production. With solar panels, for example, we can now harness enough energy to run an entire household.

The atom has been around since the beginning of time; however, humans hadn't even started harnessing this atomic energy until the mid-1800s. Hydrogen is one of the most abundant elements in the universe, but only recently has it been harnessed in a way that it can be utilized to power all sorts of machinery, including cars. The list is long when it comes to relatively recent discoveries that harness resources that have been available all along.

So how do we bridge the gap between where humankind is now and the new human or beyond human that can and will live forever?

The beginning of this answer can be found in **1 Peter 1:23 (NLT), *For you have been born again, but not to a life that will quickly end. Your new life will last forever because it comes from the eternal, living word of God.*** This was the same answer that Jesus gave a religious leader named Nicodemus when he asked him about the kingdom of heaven (John 3). Just like you and I were born of a human descent, the Good News enables us to be born again from a Divine descent.

You may have similar characteristics to your father or mother because of the genes that they carried and passed down to you. The problem is that these genes, passed on from generation to generation, have often been corrupted and, therefore, subject to decay. In the same way, the born-again person has characteristics from the gene (seed) that was passed down from the Divine One, and this gene is not subject to decay but lasts forever.

One of the core characteristics of God is being eternal! This gene or seed that comes from God is an incorruptible, non-decaying one! The goal of gene therapy parallels the gospel by attempting to make what is perishable imperishable. By protecting the telomeres from shortening, in theory, our cells should reproduce more healthy cells indefinitely. The human body is an incredible organism that contains anywhere between 50 to 75 trillion cells that are constantly regenerating themselves in various cycles.

Our stomach lining, for instance, can reproduce in less than two weeks, while skeletal muscle cells can remain around 15 years. In the same way, when we are born again, we receive a new genetic code – written by the living Word, powered by the same Spirit that raised Jesus from the dead – that begins a regeneration process in our mortal bodies, renewing us to immortal life! Peter echoes this when he refers to believers as **having been born again, not of corruptible (perishable) seed but of incorruptible (imperishable), through the word of God which lives and abides forever. 1 Peter 1:23 (NKJV).**

How serious is the Bible regarding this new divine lineage? **John 1:12-13 (NIV)** states, **Yet to all who did receive him, to those who believed in his name, he gave the right to become children of God – children born not of natural descent, nor of human decision or a husband's will, but born of God"** Salvation is a re-birth that gives us a whole new nature, genetic code, lineage, and potential for life! What a gift!

Once humans grasp the potential of this reality, there begins a renewal of the mind that transforms our thoughts, perceptions, and beliefs, which in turn affect our very biology and gene expression. In other words, the new nature starts taking shape. The modern term for this is epigenetics. Our mind is very connected to the biological processes of our bodies. A simple example is when we are under stress, adrenaline, and cortisone levels rise up in response.

In an emergency or life-threatening circumstance, this is a good thing, but only when it's temporal. When cortisone and other stress hormones stay at elevated levels over time, they disrupt almost all functions. The body's immune, digestive and reproductive systems, as well as growth processes, are all negatively affected.

Consequently then, constant worry and anxiety create a toxic chemical environment in your body, which enables corruption. This is why the Word tells us in **Matthew 6:25 (NIV), Therefore I tell you, do not worry about your life, what you will eat or drink; or about your body, what you will wear. Is not life more than food and the body more than clothes?** Rather than dwelling on fear, the apostle Paul says what we should keep our minds on; **Since you have been raised to new life with Christ, set your sights on the realities of heaven, where Christ sits in the place of honor at God's right hand. Think about the things in heaven, not the things of earth. Colossians 3:1-2 (NLT).**

In heaven, there is perfect peace, prosperity, and harmony. In heaven, there is only eternal love and grace. Heaven is where immortality already dwells. When many people think of heaven, there is a tendency to spiritualize all aspects, and it's easy to forget the biblical truth that Jesus himself was raised from the dead in a physical body and that he was taken into heaven in a physical body. We see this in **Luke 24:36-43 (NLT),** when the disciples were gathered telling of their experiences after Jesus' resurrection, **and just as they were telling about it, Jesus himself was suddenly standing there among them. "Peace be with you," he said. But the whole group was startled and frightened, thinking they were seeing a ghost! "Why are you frightened?" He asked. "Why are your hearts filled with doubt? Look at my hands. Look at my feet. You can see that it's really me. Touch me and make sure that I am not a ghost, because ghosts don't have bodies, as you see that I do." As he** *spoke, he showed them his hands and his feet. Still they stood there in disbelief, filled with joy and wonder. Then he asked them, "Do you have anything here to eat?" They gave him a piece of broiled fish, and he ate it as they watched.*

To further evidence his physical resurrection, **Acts 1:9-11 (NIV)** explains it. **After he said this, he was taken up before their very eyes, and a cloud hid him from their sight. They were looking intently up into the sky as he was going when suddenly two men dressed in white spotted beside them. "Men of Galilee," they said, "why do you stand here looking here into the sky? This same Jesus, who has been taken from you into heaven, will come back in the same way you have seen him go into heaven.**

Jesus was certainly raised into a physical body, but not the same one he died in. He was raised into an imperishable physical body that was no longer subject to death and decay! It's imperative that we understand this concept of a transformed physical body if we are to ever believe (let alone realize) immortality while living on earth. Let's journey into Paul's teaching, with the understanding that he is speaking to the church of Corinth about resurrection for those who have already died:

So will it be with the resurrection of the dead? The body that is sown is perishable; it is raised imperishable; it is sown in dishonor; it is raised in glory; it is sown in weakness; it is raised in power; it is sown a natural body, it is raised a spiritual body. If there is a natural body, there is also a spiritual body. So it is written: "the first man Adam became a living being"; the last Adam (meaning Christ), a life-giving spirit. The spiritual did not come first, but the natural and after that, the spiritual. The first man was of the dust of the earth; the second man (Christ) is of heaven. As was the earthly man, so are those who are of the earth; and as is the heavenly man, so also are those who are of heaven. And just as we have borne the image of the earthly man, so shall we bear the image of the heavenly man. 1 Corinthians

15:42-49 (NIV).

Let me sum up what Paul is saying. The "first Adam" – humanity in its natural state – dies, but the "last Adam" is a heavenly being that is not subject to death or decay. However, this heavenly body is not just some ethereal ghost or floating spirit, but an actual body with a substance that can do far above and beyond what we can imagine. Because we were born from human descent, we have borne the image of the first Adam. But once we are born again from above (heaven), born of God (by the way, this is why we call God "our Father"), we will bear the image of the last Adam, who is Christ. You see, Christ came from God and took on the earthly human image so that we can partake of his heavenly image. **Romans 6:5-10 (NIV)** reveals, ***For if we have been united with him in a death like his, we will certainly also be united with him in a resurrection like his. For we know that our old self was crucified with him so that the body ruled by sin (death) might be done away with, that we should no longer be slaves to sin – because anyone who has died has been set free from sin. Now, if we died with Christ, we believe that we will also live with him. For we know that since Christ was raised from the dead, he cannot die again; death no longer has mastery over him. The death he died, he died to sin once for all; but the life he lives, he lives to God.***

To Die or Not to Die

Before I take you a bit further in 1 Corinthians 15, I would be expedient to briefly explain some general principles regarding bible translation technic, as it will deepen your understanding of the next verses. Some bible translation uses what they call a "formal equivalence," which is a word for word or literal translation. Others use a more "dynamic equivalence," which is more of a sense for sense translation, meaning that whole phrases or sentences are translated to convey the meaning with readability in mind. And some translations range between the two approaches.

For example, our current language uses an idiom that goes something like, "it's raining cats and dogs." If we translated that with the formal equivalence, it would be translated, "it's raining cats and dogs." If it was translated using dynamic equivalence, it would probably read something like, "it's raining very heavily." Both translation methods have their advantages and disadvantages, that's why I recommend reading from as many different translations as possible.

In 1 Corinthians 15:50, the NIV uses formal equivalence to translate the Greek words "sarx and haima" to "flesh and blood," while the NLT translates with the dynamic equivalence to "physical bodies." However, in this case, the dynamic equivalent can be misleading because it overlooks the reality that our spiritual bodies are physical as well. For this reason, I want to look at the next verses from a combination of versions:

I declare to you, brothers and sisters, that flesh and blood cannot inherit the kingdom of God. These dying bodies cannot inherit what will last forever. But let me reveal to you a wonderful secret. We will not all die, but we will all be transformed! It will happen in a moment, in the blink of an eye, when the last trumpet is blown. For when the trumpet sounds, those who have died will be raised to live forever. And we who are living will also be transformed. For our dying bodies must be transformed into bodies that will never die; our mortal bodies must be transformed into immortal bodies." 1 Cor. 15:50-53 (NIV/NLT). What's this text saying? That there will be people who have already died who will be raised to immortal life and those that are still living that will be transformed into an immortal life. I prefer the latter, don't you? There's another account in the Bible that confirms this very thing. Although there are several biblical accounts of Jesus raising people from the dead. Let's turn our attention to the raising of Lazarus.

While Jesus was approaching the place where Lazarus was buried, Lazarus's sister Martha came out to meet him, and part of their discourse is found in ***John 11:25-26 (AMPC), Jesus said to her, "I am [Myself] the***

Resurrection and the Life. Whoever believes in (adheres to, trusts in, and relies on) Me, although he may die, yet he shall live; And whoever continues to live and believes in (has faith in, cleaves to, and relies on) Me shall never [actually] die at all. Do you believe this?"

Jesus is saying that those who die will be resurrected into new imperishable bodies, and those who are alive can be transformed into imperishable bodies (without dying first). Jesus himself actually demonstrated both options before he was crucified! He was transfigured into a heavenly body (while on earth), then back into a human body so he could die and be resurrected into his heavenly body. Accounts of his transfiguration are found in the synoptic gospels (Matthew, Mark, and Luke) but also eluded to in John and 2 Peter.

Six days later, Jesus took Peter and the two brothers, James and John, and led them up a high mountain to be alone. As the men watched, Jesus' appearance was transformed so that his face shone like the sun, and his clothes became as white as light. Suddenly, Moses and Elijah appeared and began talking with Jesus. Matthew 17:1-3 (NLT).

Jesus was revealing the perfection of life in the heavenly body. His glory was being revealed to such a degree that the heavenly dimension opened up around him and Moses and Elijah appeared standing with him. The idea that this was his "imperishable body" is confirmed several decades later, long after the resurrection of Jesus and his ascension into heaven, when we find John imprisoned on the island of Patmos.

One Sunday, he was in the spirit, and he saw a heavenly vision of Jesus that is similar to what Jesus looked like on the mountain when he transformed before his disciples. John's description (found in Revelation 1:16) entails the image that Jesus' face was shining like the sun in all its brilliance. We can conclude that on the mountain of transfiguration, Jesus' mortal body was transformed into an immortal heavenly body and then back to his mortal body so that he could willingly lay down his life by crucifixion.

Jesus broke the curse of sin and death over mankind when the Spirit raised him into a new, immortal being. We are invited to be partakers in this imperishable life through transformation by the same Spirit! One of the most well-known prayers Jesus taught his disciples to pray, ***Our Father in heaven, hallowed by your name, your kingdom come, your will be done, on earth as it is in heaven. Matthew 6:9-10 (NIV).*** Since heaven is a place of eternity and immortality, should come as no surprise that it is God's will and purpose to bring heaven (immortality) to earth, and Jesus is the means to fulfill his perfect will.

> Whoever **BELIEVES** in **HIM**
>
> Shall **NOT PERISH**
>
> But have **EVERLASTING** Life
>
> **John 3:16 (NIV)**

Not the End but the Beginning

For those of us that are still alive today (I'm assuming you are since you are reading this book), we are left with a few options moving forward. We can throw out the science and possibility that we are wired for eternal life and go on unchanged (red pill, anyone!?). Or, we can acknowledge the possibility of immortality and put our hope in ever-advancing technology and scientific authority in anticipation of the next medical breakthrough in immortality.

We can invest our time and extensive resources to that end (not to mention invasive therapies), or we can embrace a third option that has been paid in full by Christ himself. We can submit ourselves to the highest authority and access immortal life that's been available to us this whole time through faith in Jesus Christ. We can choose not to conform to the system (death) of this world but to be transformed by the renewing of our minds – by seeing Jesus and the Good News in the glorious light that it was meant to be seen in. If we have been "born again" as a child of God, we can start accessing the eternal realm where the power of immortality is made available to those who believe right here on earth. God's imperishable seed can begin working in us!

You might ask what if it doesn't work? A fair question, but allow me to ask you a few questions to ponder in return. What if believing the good news only added 5 more years of quality, healthy living to your life? Would it still be worth believing?

Consider the alternative – remaining in the same mindset and living a life that its certain end is death (although even IF we die, we confidently know we will be raised into a gloriously transformed body). I believe that even if we only experience a partial manifestation of eternal life that comes from God in this lifetime, it's worth it to embark on this journey of faith and embrace the full gospel of Jesus Christ – an eternal life lived in union with our creator, with his precious spirit indwelling, empowering, and renewing our minds and bodied towards life.

Although it's taken scientists and mankind generations to realize what God's word has pointed to all along, it's incredible to realize that we truly are created in the image of God; he knit us together, even down to a cellular level, to reflect his glory and immortality. He inscribed his imperishable truth within our DNA, creating us with the genetic potential to live eternally in union with him. When death reigned over mankind, he sacrificed his own Son to conquer it and restore life and immortality to us. All this is made possible because of the incredible love of God for His creation. Along this journey of a never-ending life, He couples it with His peace and joy so that we can live an abundant life indeed.

But if the Spirit of Him who raised Jesus from the dead dwells in you, He who raised Christ from the dead will also give life to your mortal bodies through His Spirit who dwells in you. Romans 8:11(NKJV).

Do you believe?

Citations

[1] ft.com, Andrew Jack March 5th, 2020 - https://www.ft.com/content/f61f8cf8-2274-11ea-b8a1-584213ee7b2b

[2] https://brightside.me/wonder-curiosities/5-ways-we-can-become-immortal-according-to-modern-science-and-reasons-were-not-immortal-yet-441760/

[3] https://nypost.com/2018/01/06/scientists-could-one-day-make-humans-immortal/

[4] https://www.ted.com/speakers/aubrey_de_grey

Literature

[1] eLife 2018;7:e31157 DOI: 10.7554/eLife.31157

ABOUT THE AUTHOR

Sylvie is a prolific writer and author of different inspirational devotionals and books, including a children's book, Lilly and Willy Dilly - God is love. She is an articulate Editor of the daily publication, Your E-Word, (Your Encouraging Word). Her zeal for the Lord is not limited to the church walls, but she's been passionately involved in the Marketplace ministry for over twenty years. She's unapologetically open to the move of God at all times, even when it means plying the path less traveled.

Sylvie continuously thrives on witnessing the truth of the gospel and seeing people filled with eternal joy. She loves to minister and encourage people of all ages (children and adults) on God's amazing love.

When she's not engaged in the corporate world, or on specific ministry assignments, you will find her with her family.

Presently, she lives in Florida with her loving husband of over thirty years, and their marriage is blessed with two adult children, their spouses and grandchildren.

You can contact Sylvie on her website at www.yourEword.com.

You can also sign up to receive her free daily E-Word. It is similar to the messages in this book. You will find it encouraging and it will empower you to receive more truths and set you free, to enjoy your life at a new level.

Made in the USA
Columbia, SC
01 July 2025

60194222R00085